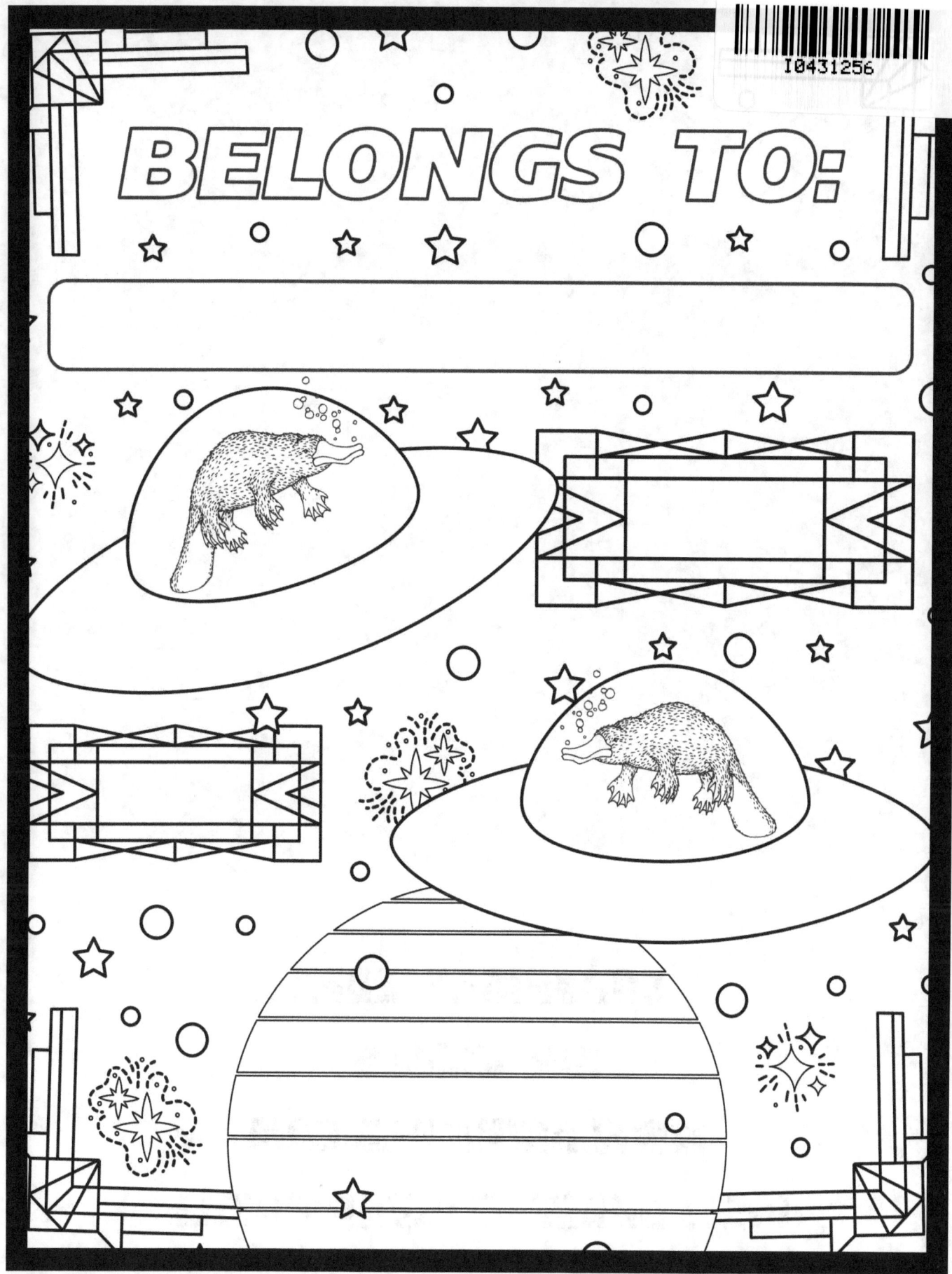

COPYRIGHT 2022
ADI NICOLE
WWW.ADINICOLE.COM
INSTAGRAM: @THEADINICOLE

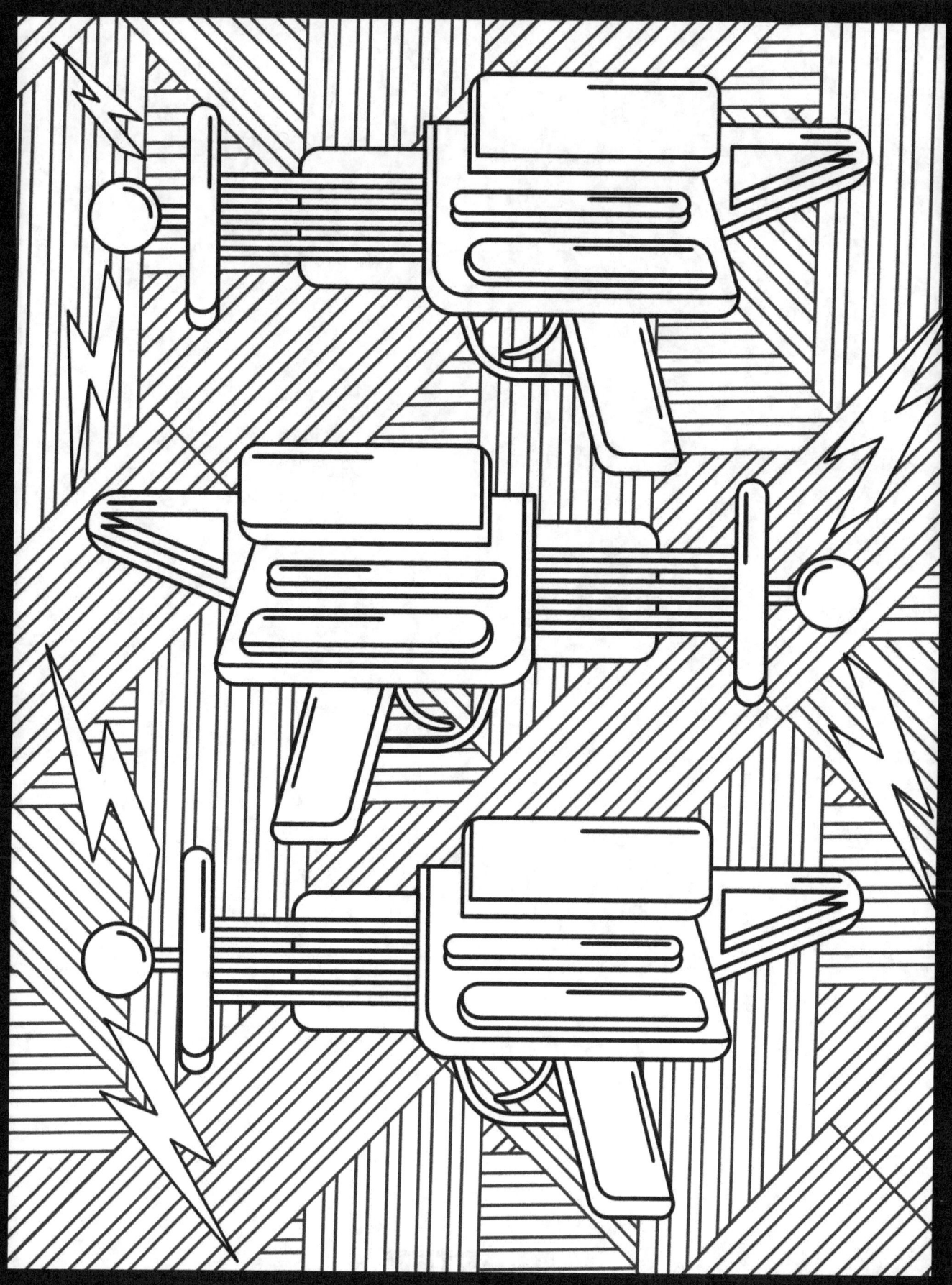

BLASTED

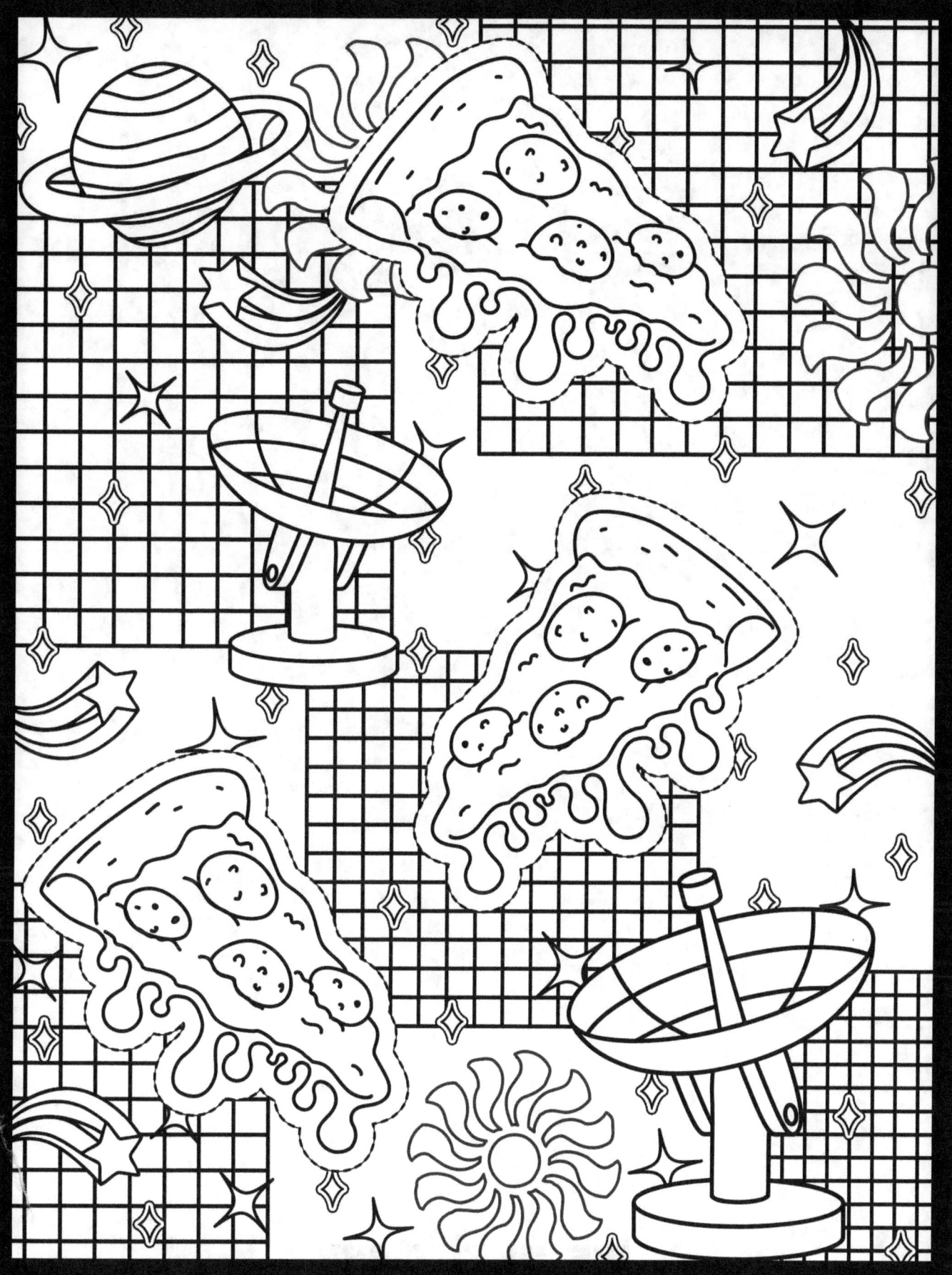

PIE IN THE SKY

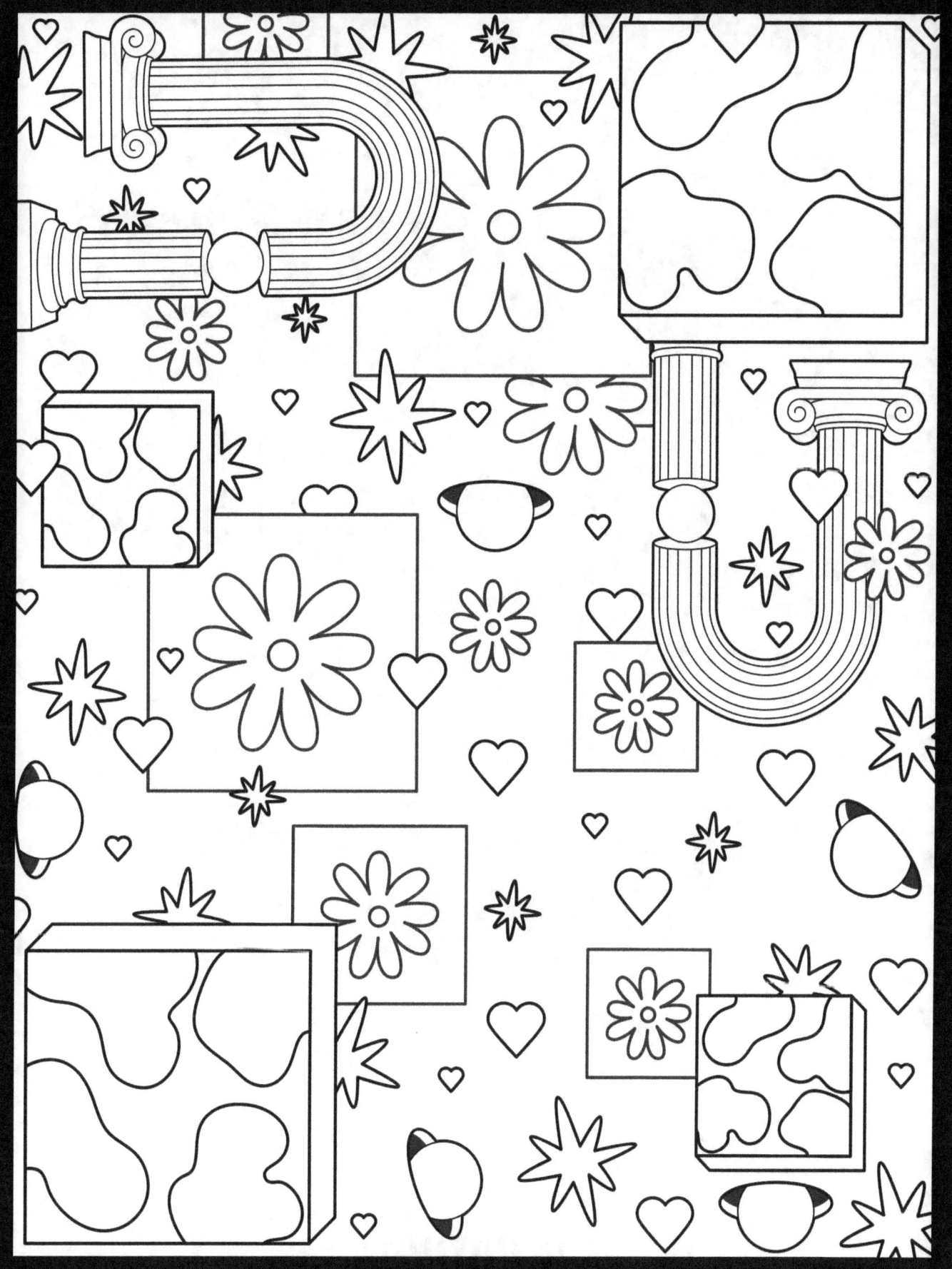

FLOATING

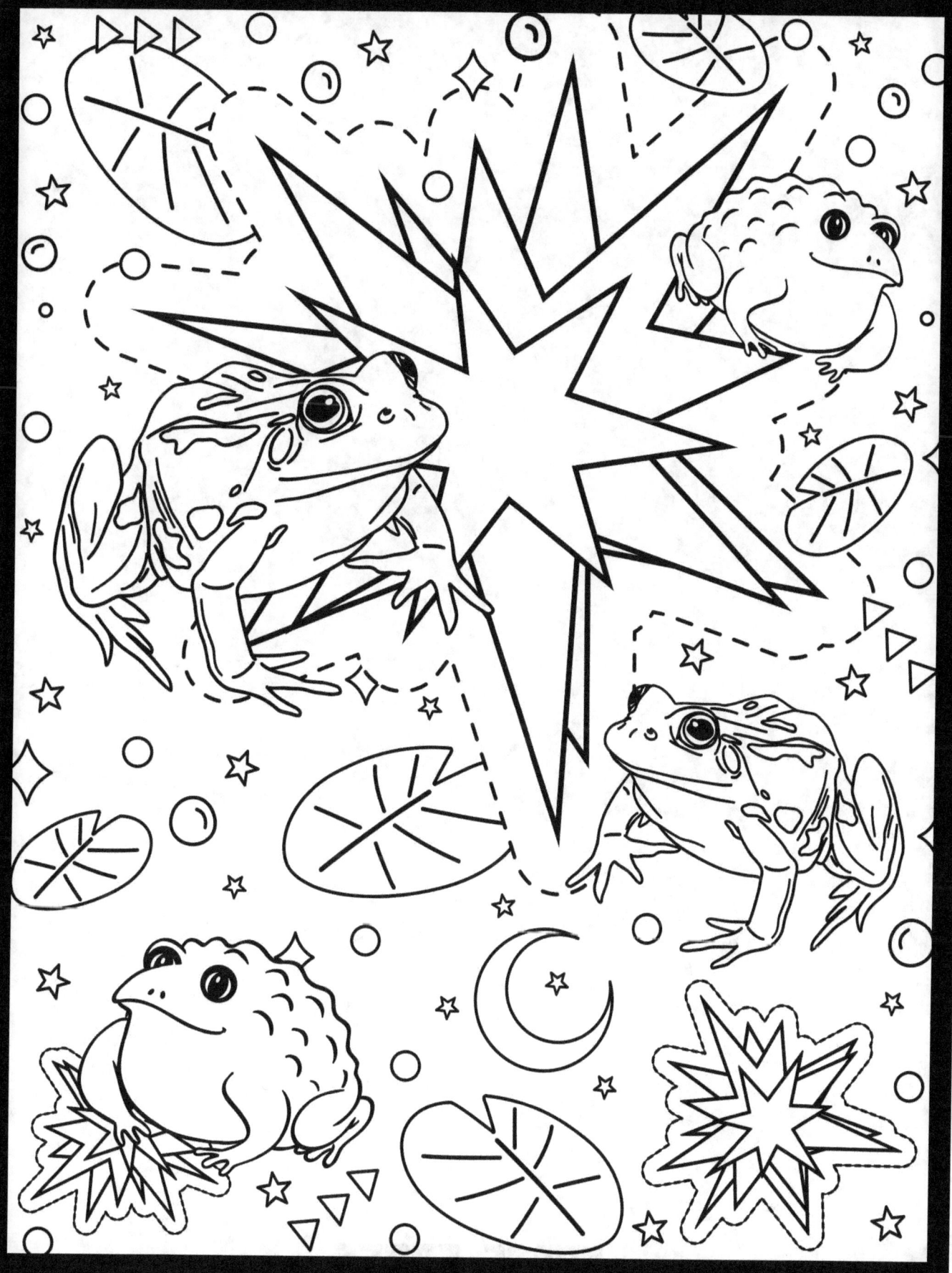

SPACE FROGS

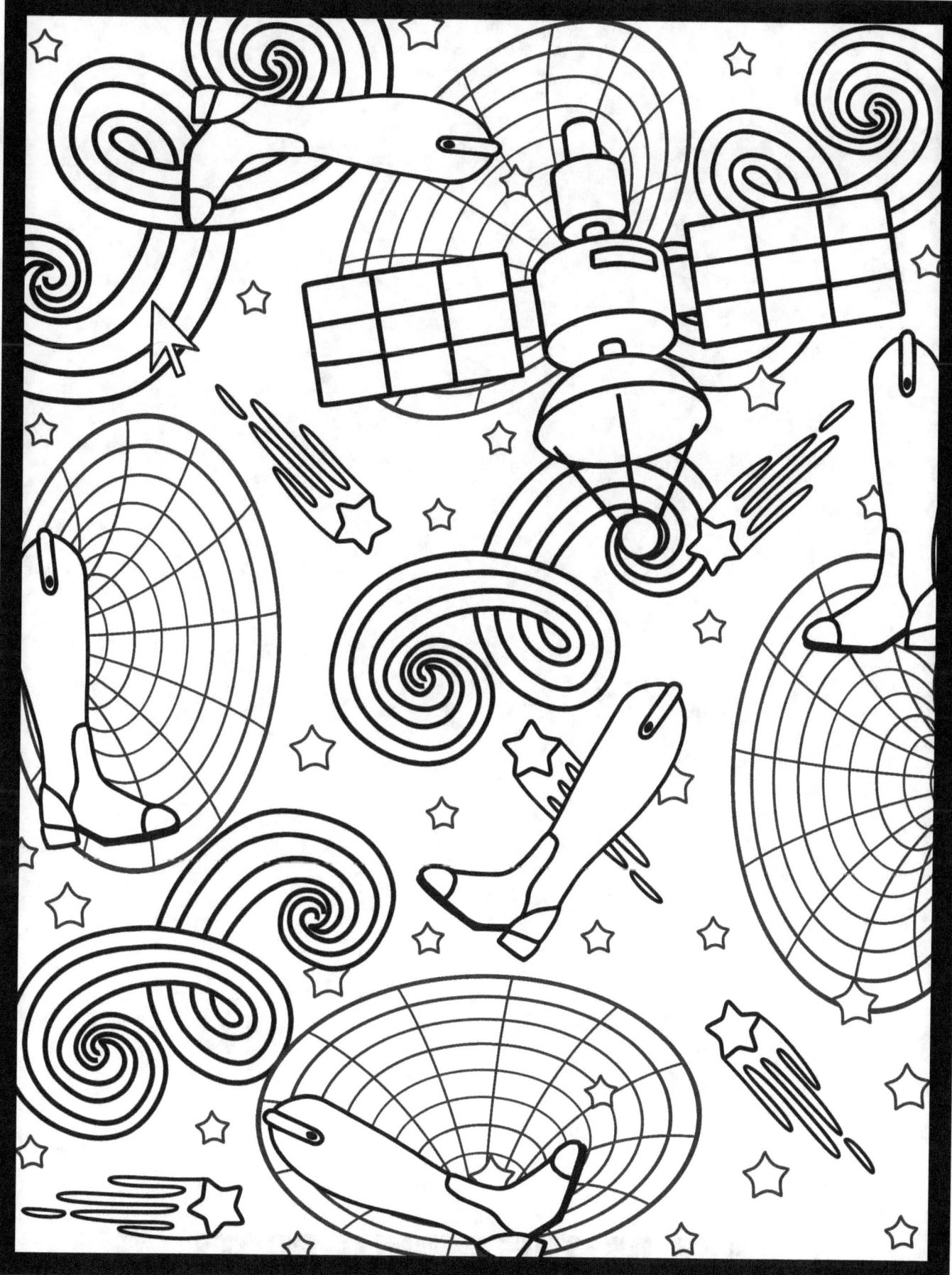

OUT OF THIS WORLD BOOTS

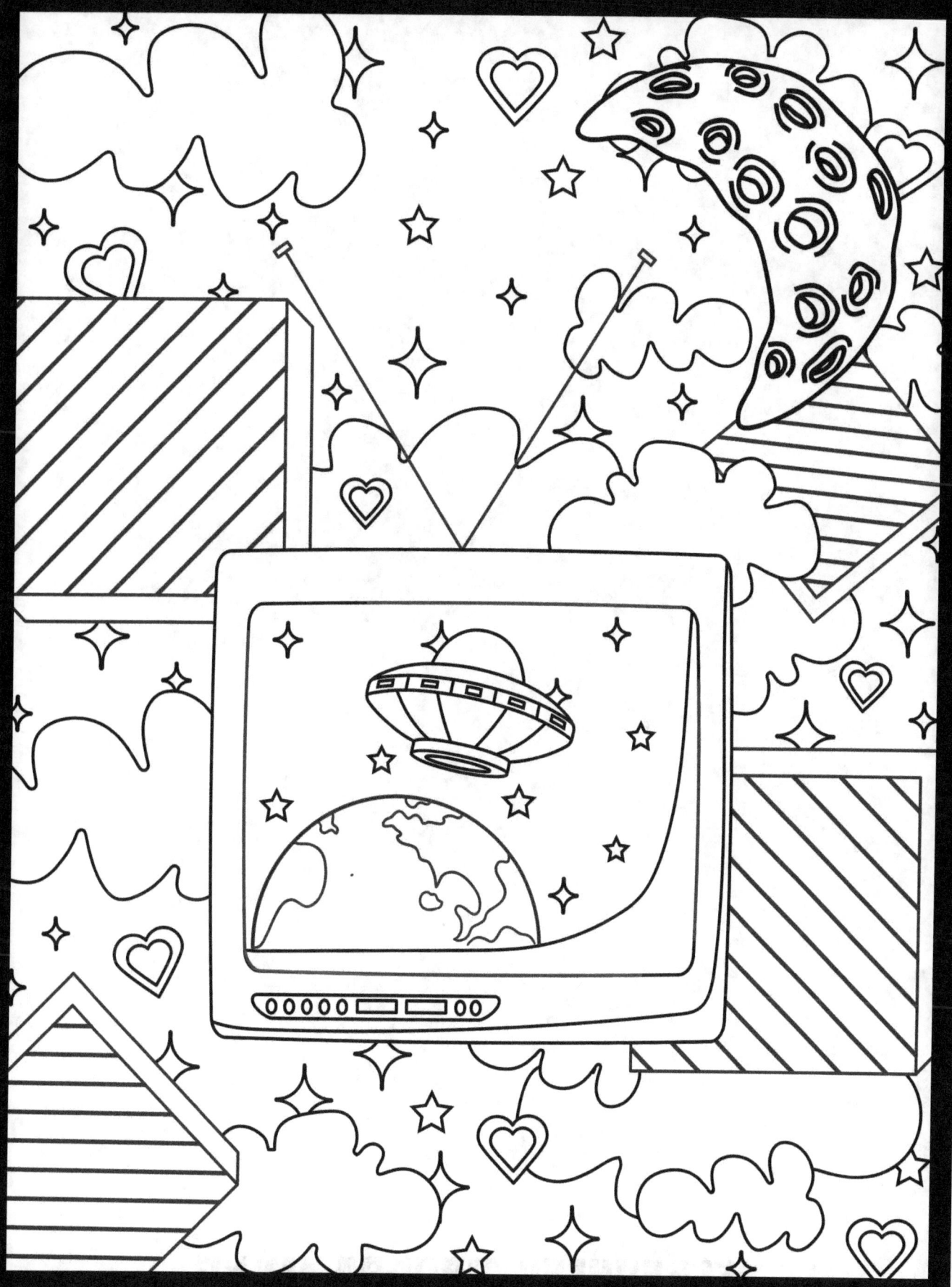

SCHEDULED PROGRAMMING

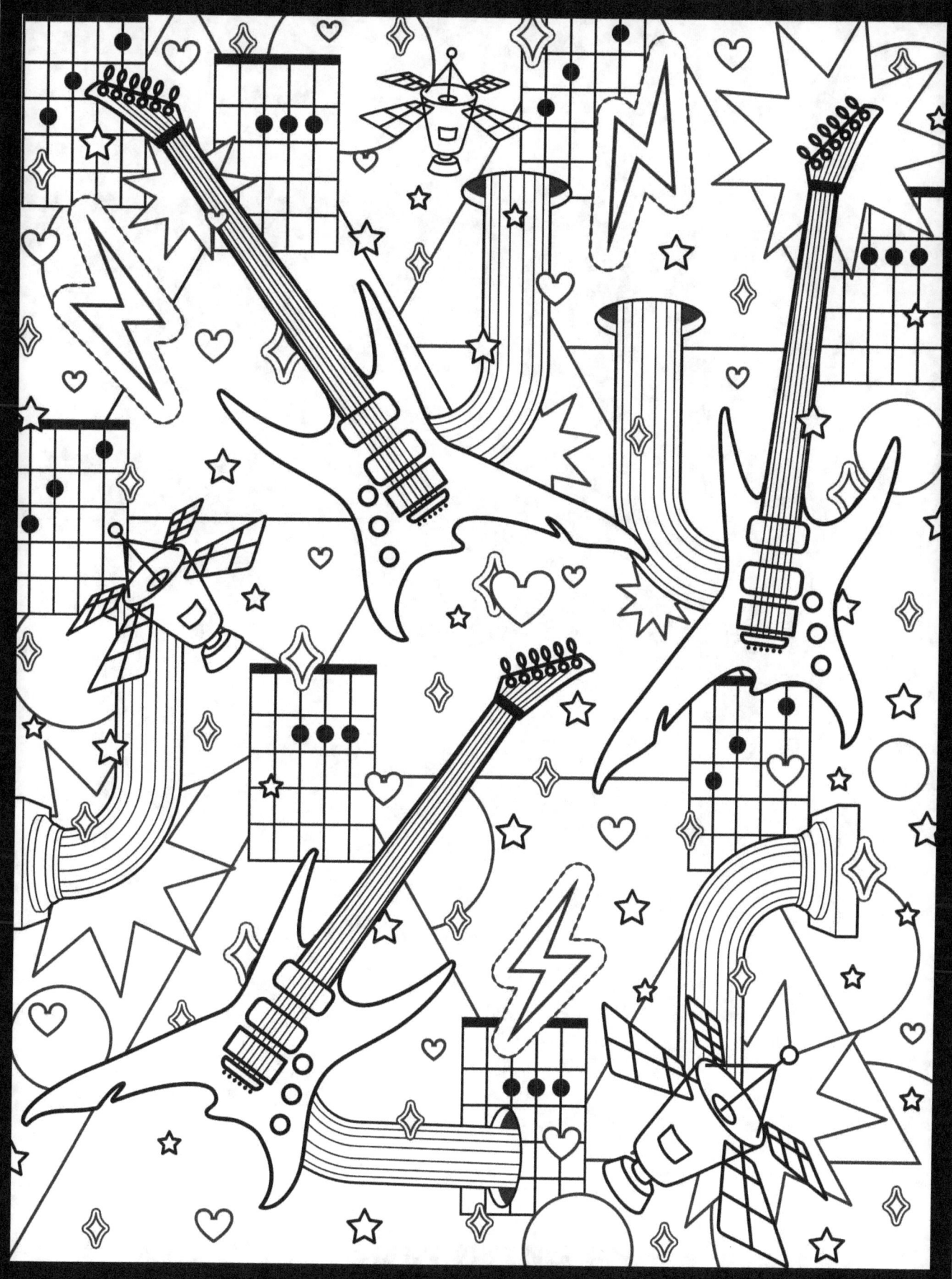

ROCKSTAR

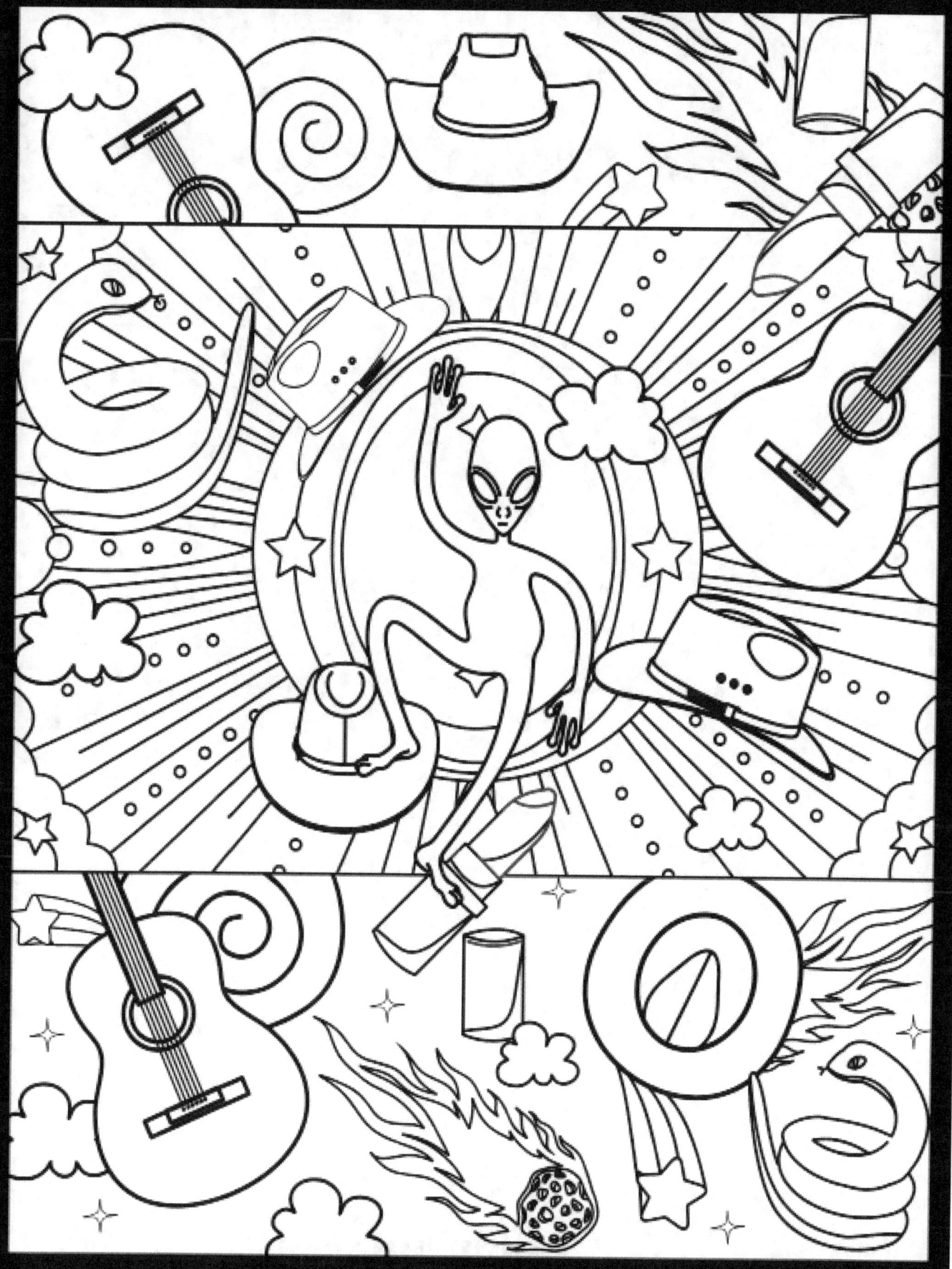

GIDDY UP

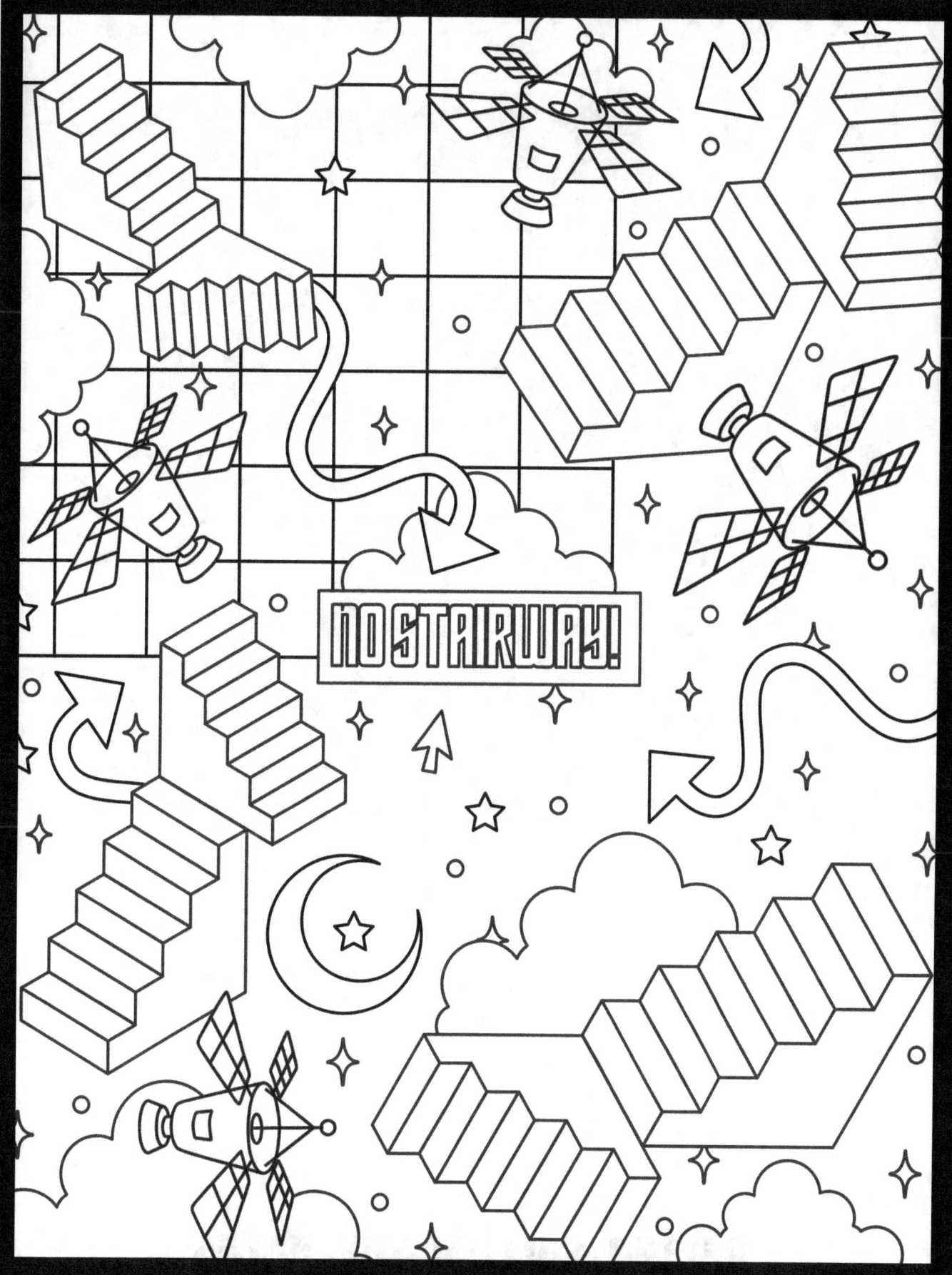

BETTER FOLLOW THE RULES

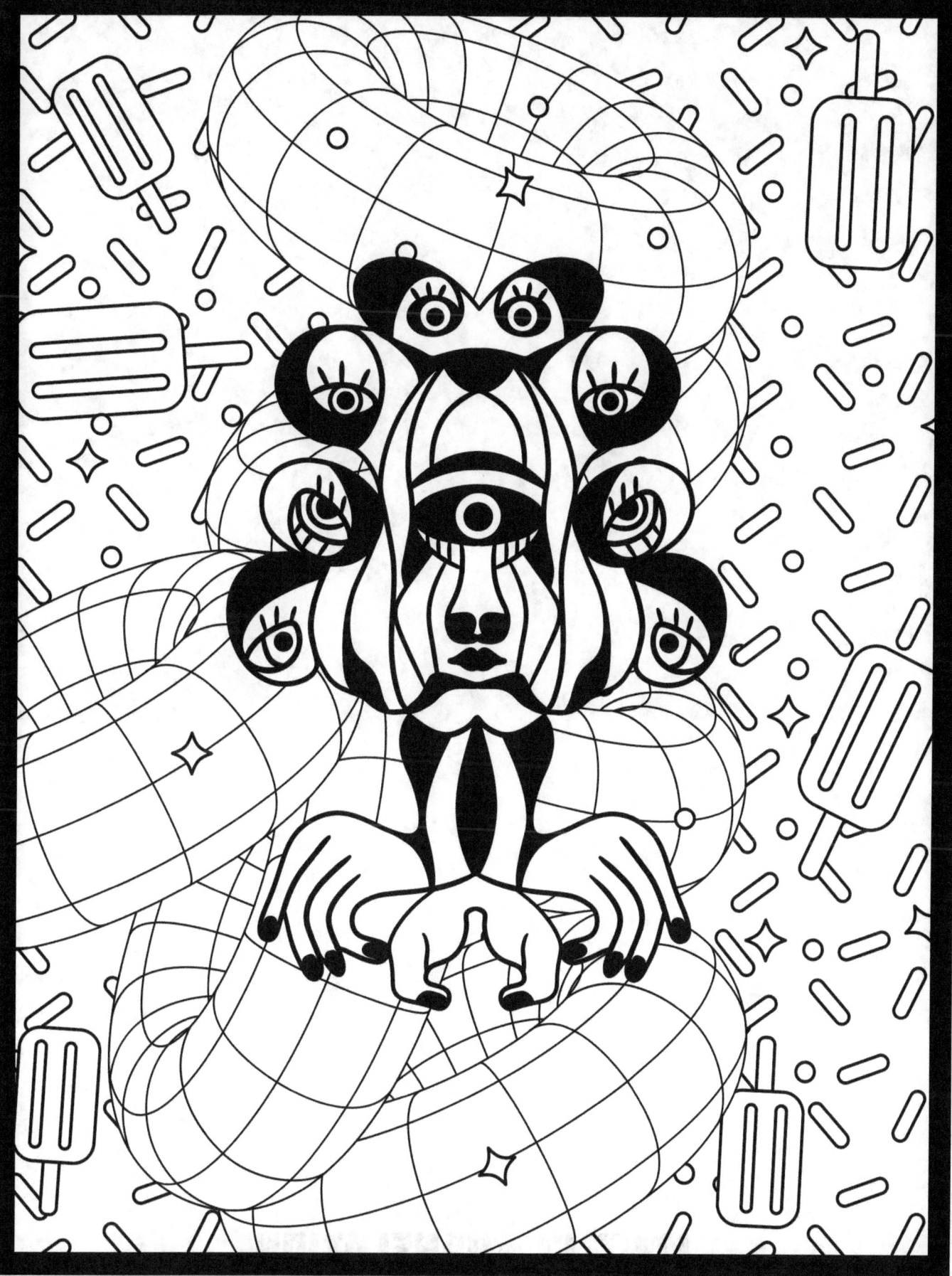

LOST IN TRANSLATION

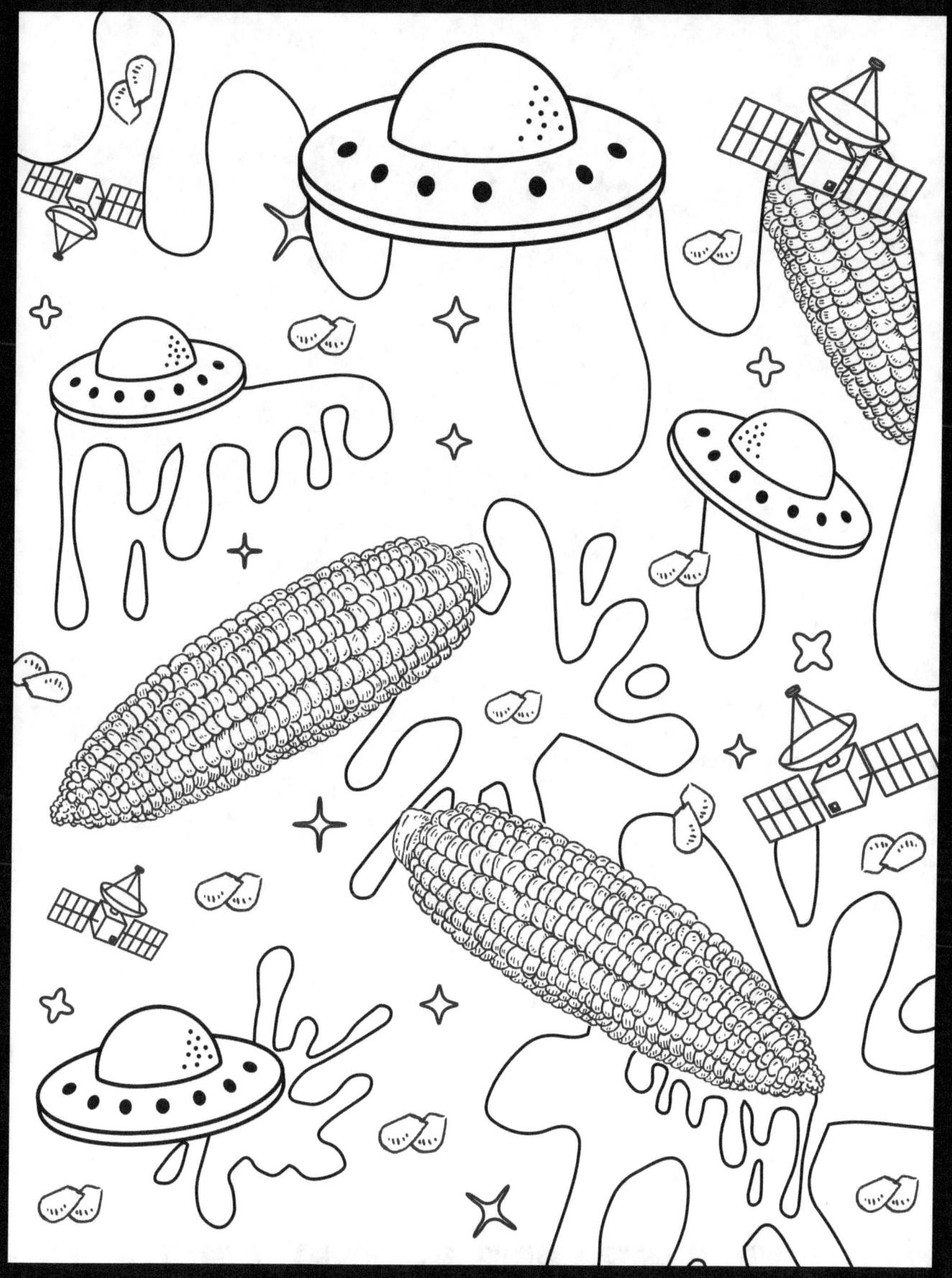

SAVE ME SOME OF THAT CORN

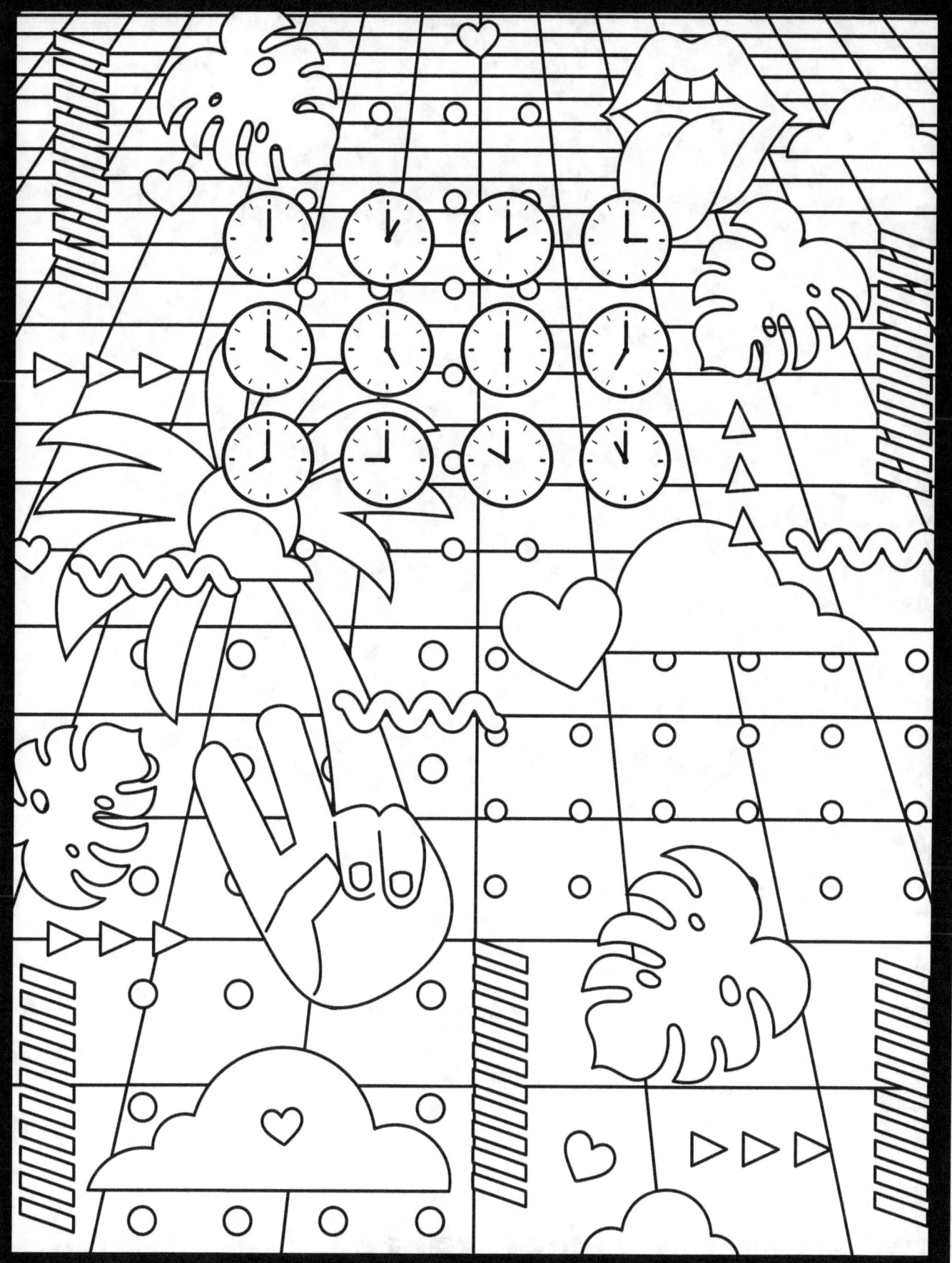

FAST TRACK

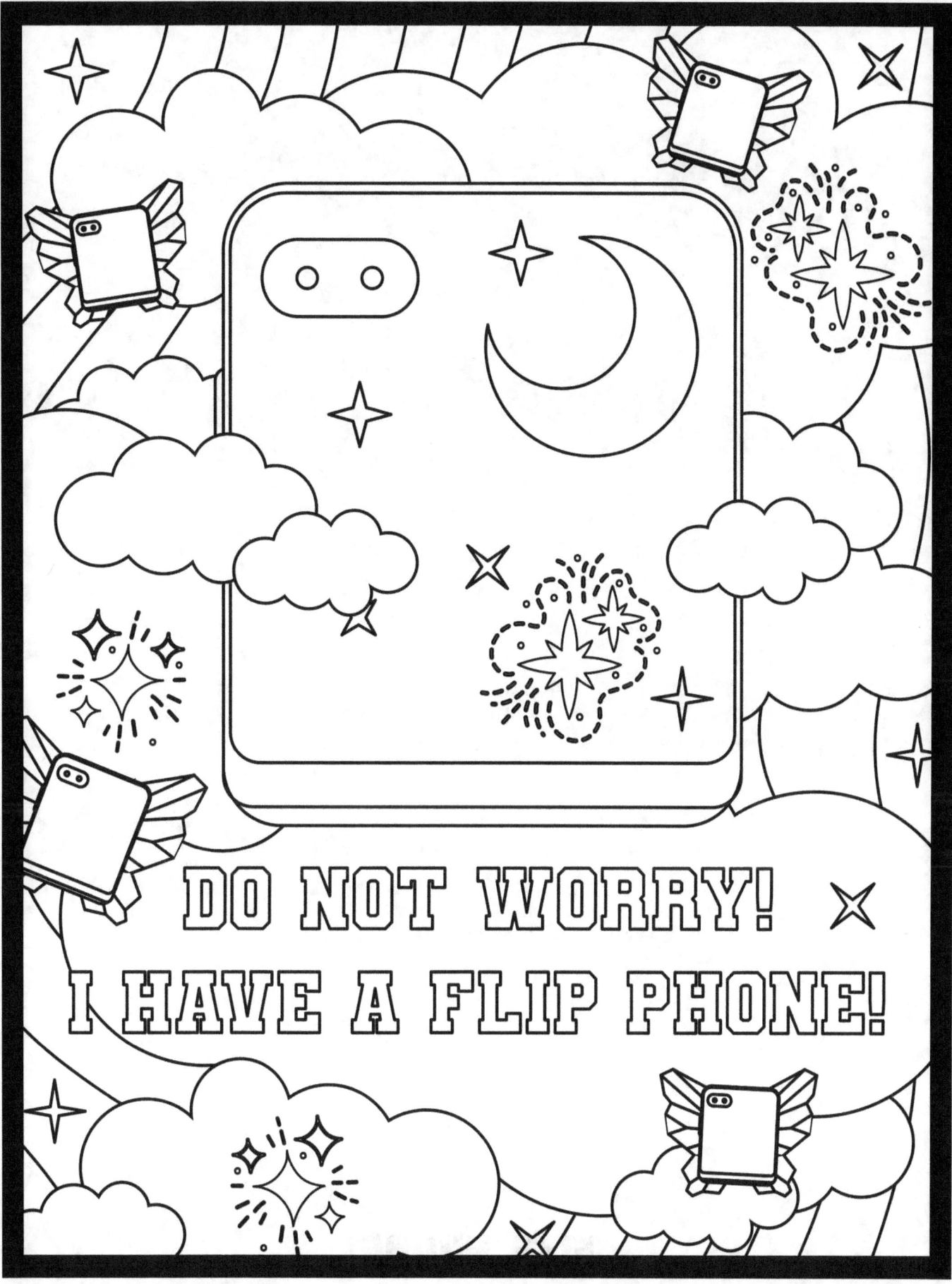

FLIP PHONE

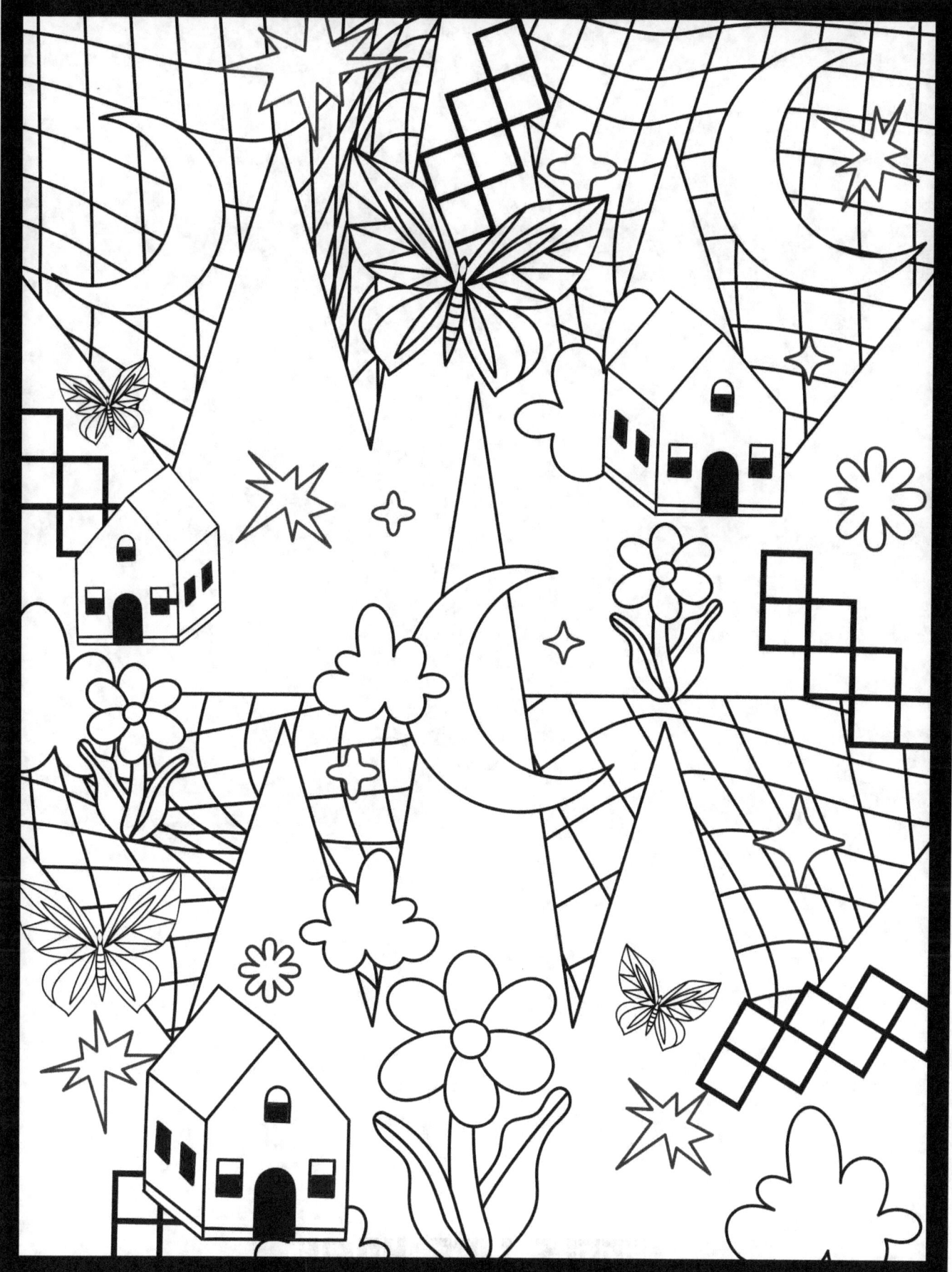

FEELS LIKE HOME

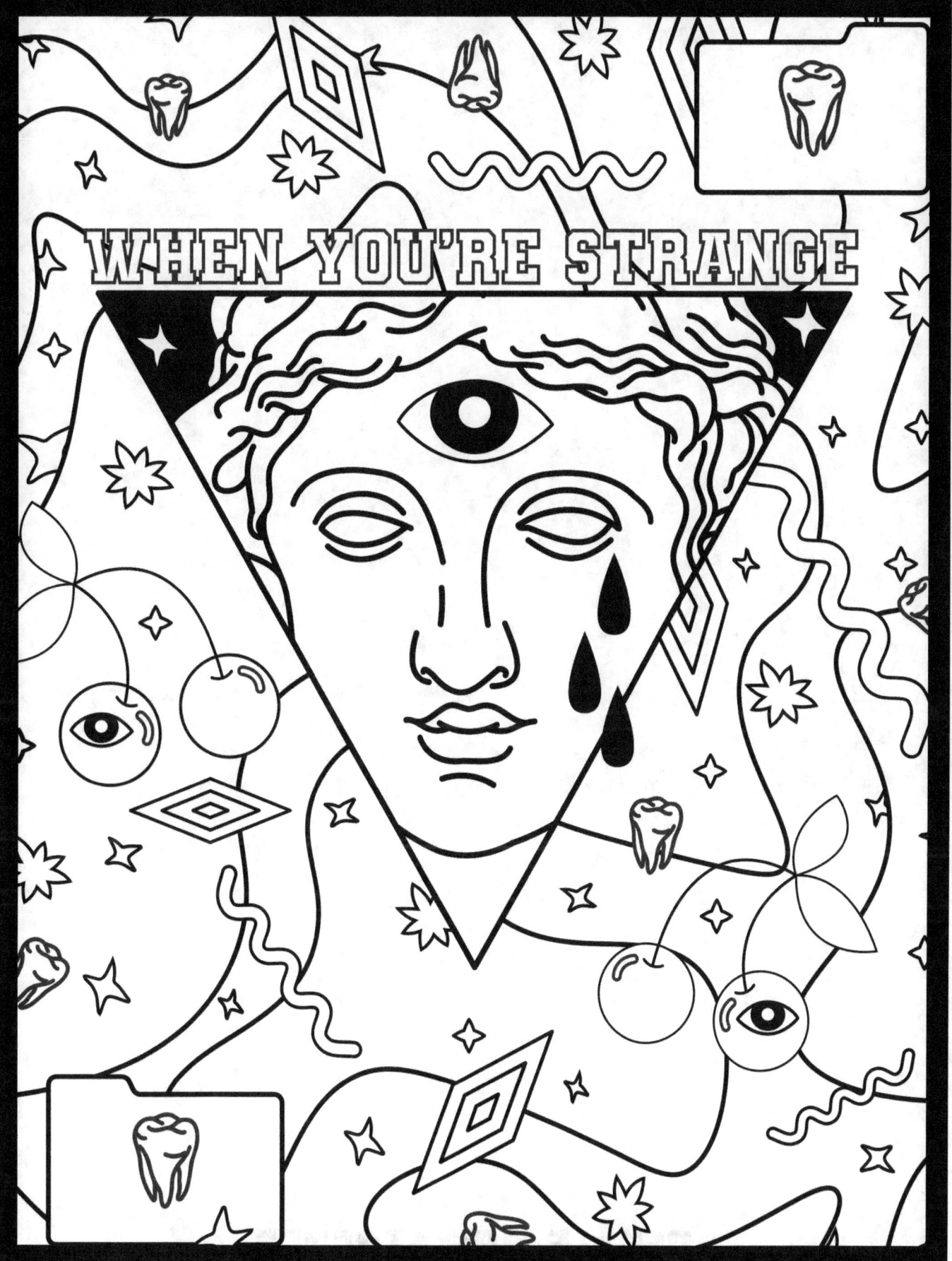

PEOPLE ARE STRANGE

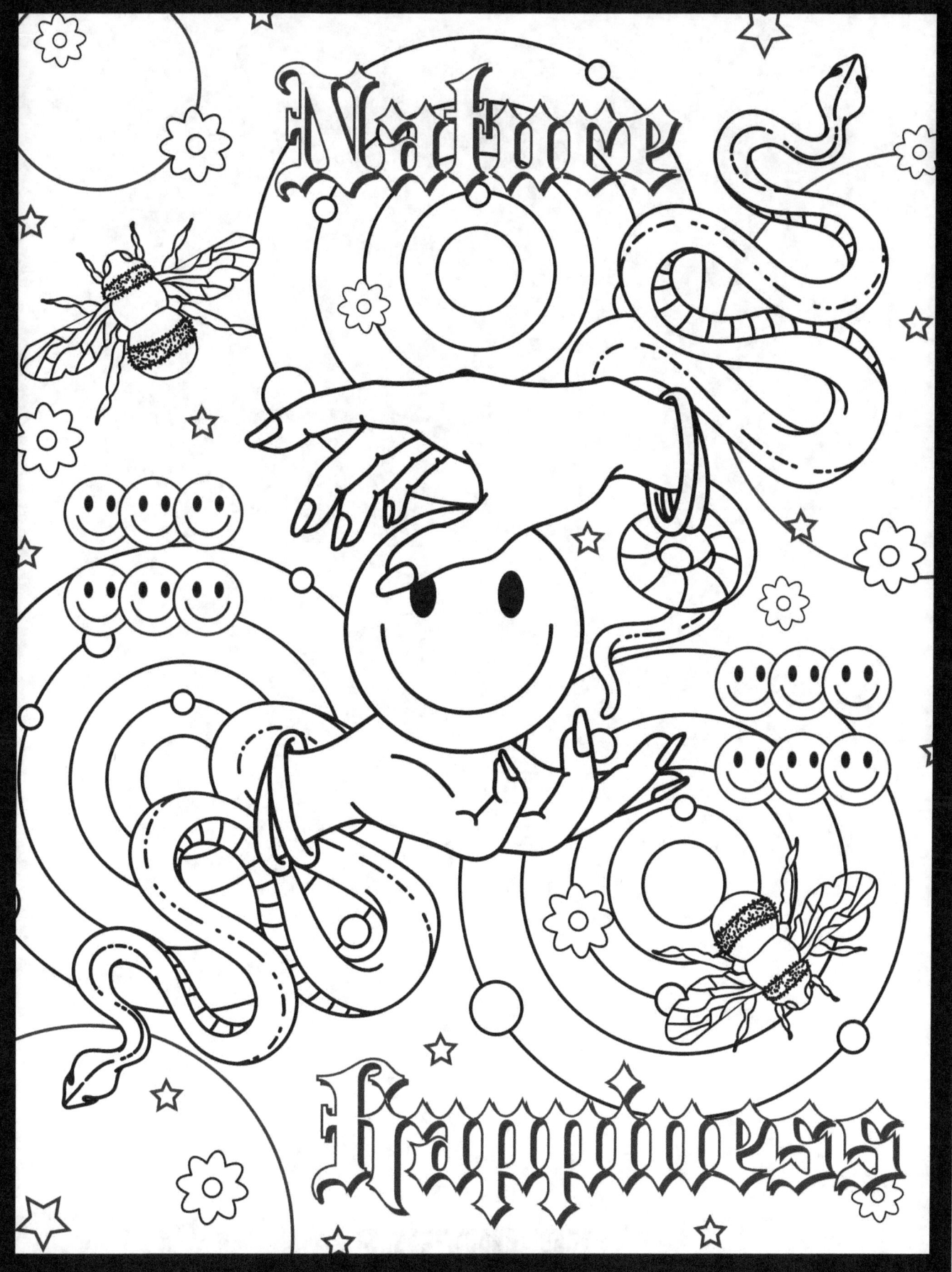

GO OUTSIDE

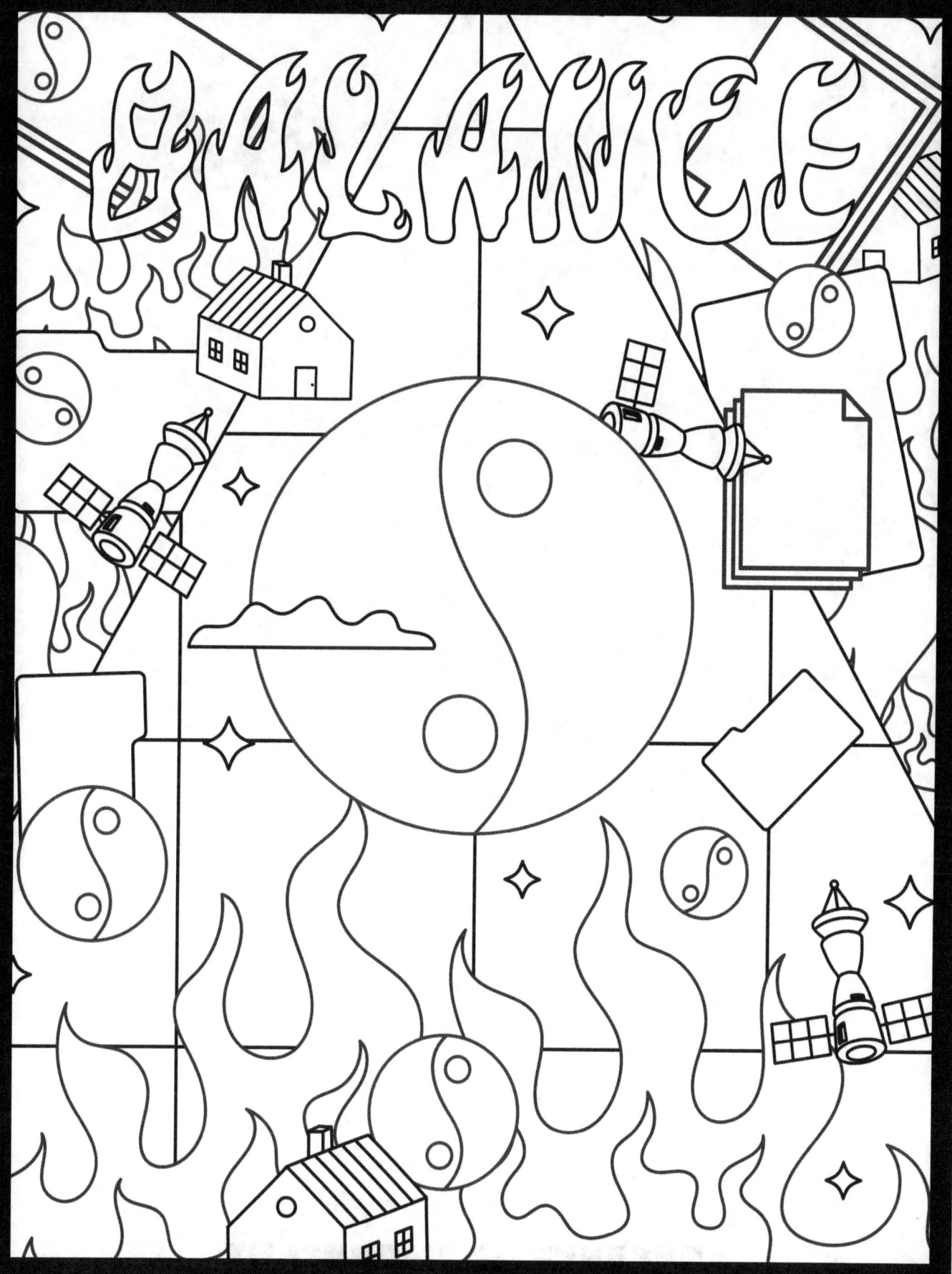

BALANCE IS IMPORTANT

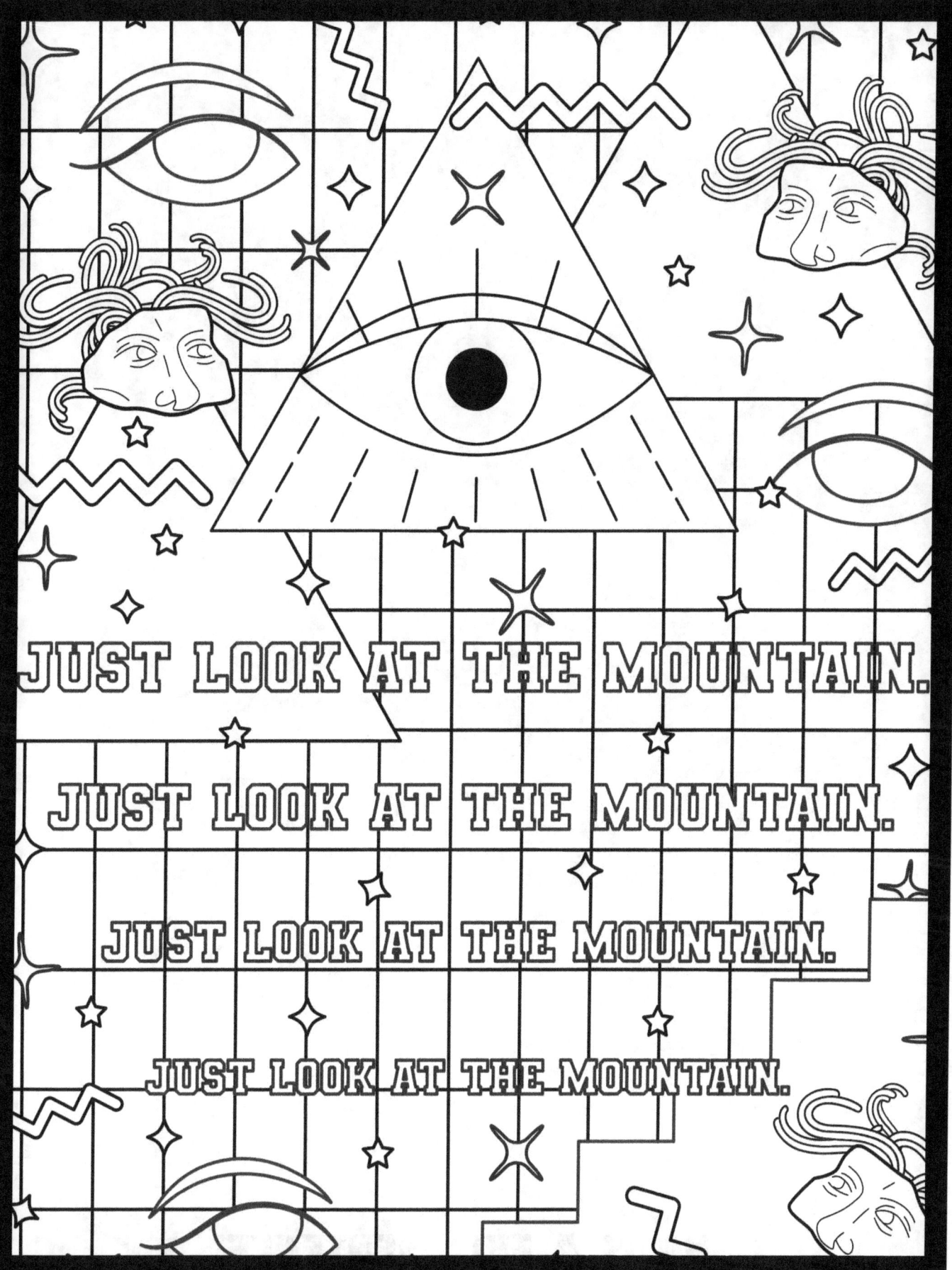

NO IS A FULL SENTENCE

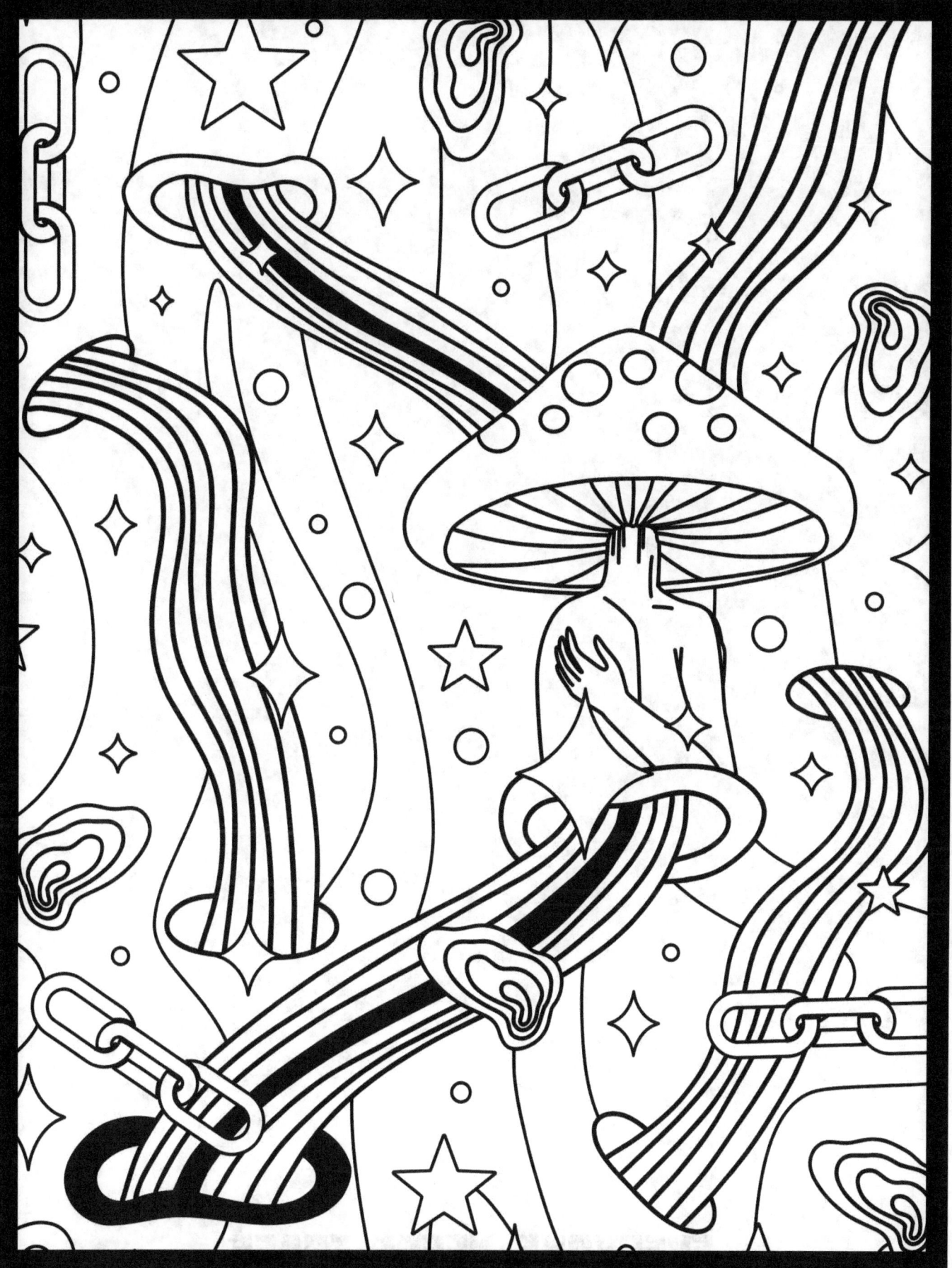

EVERYONE NEEDS SPACE

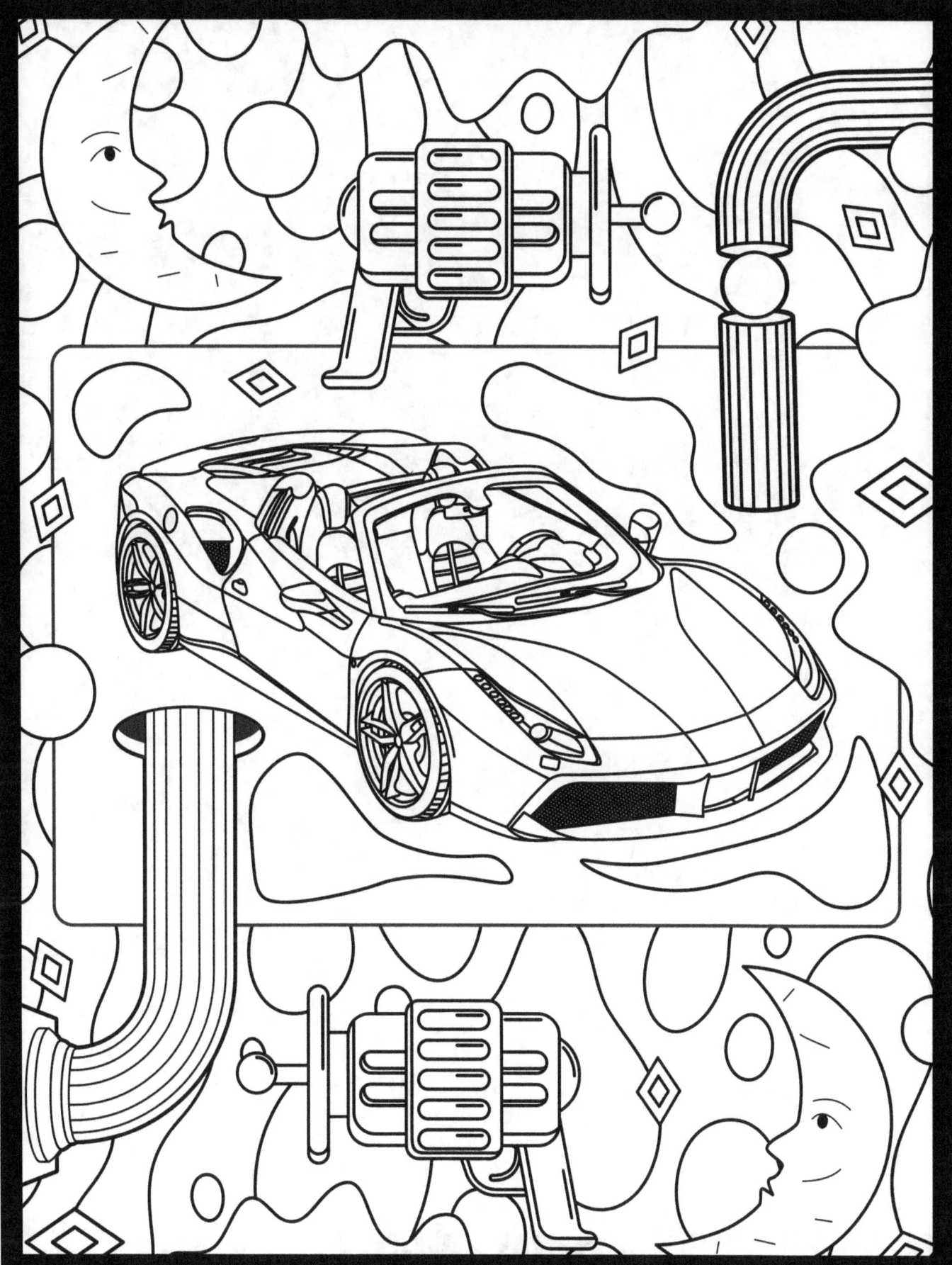

ZOOM MOONS

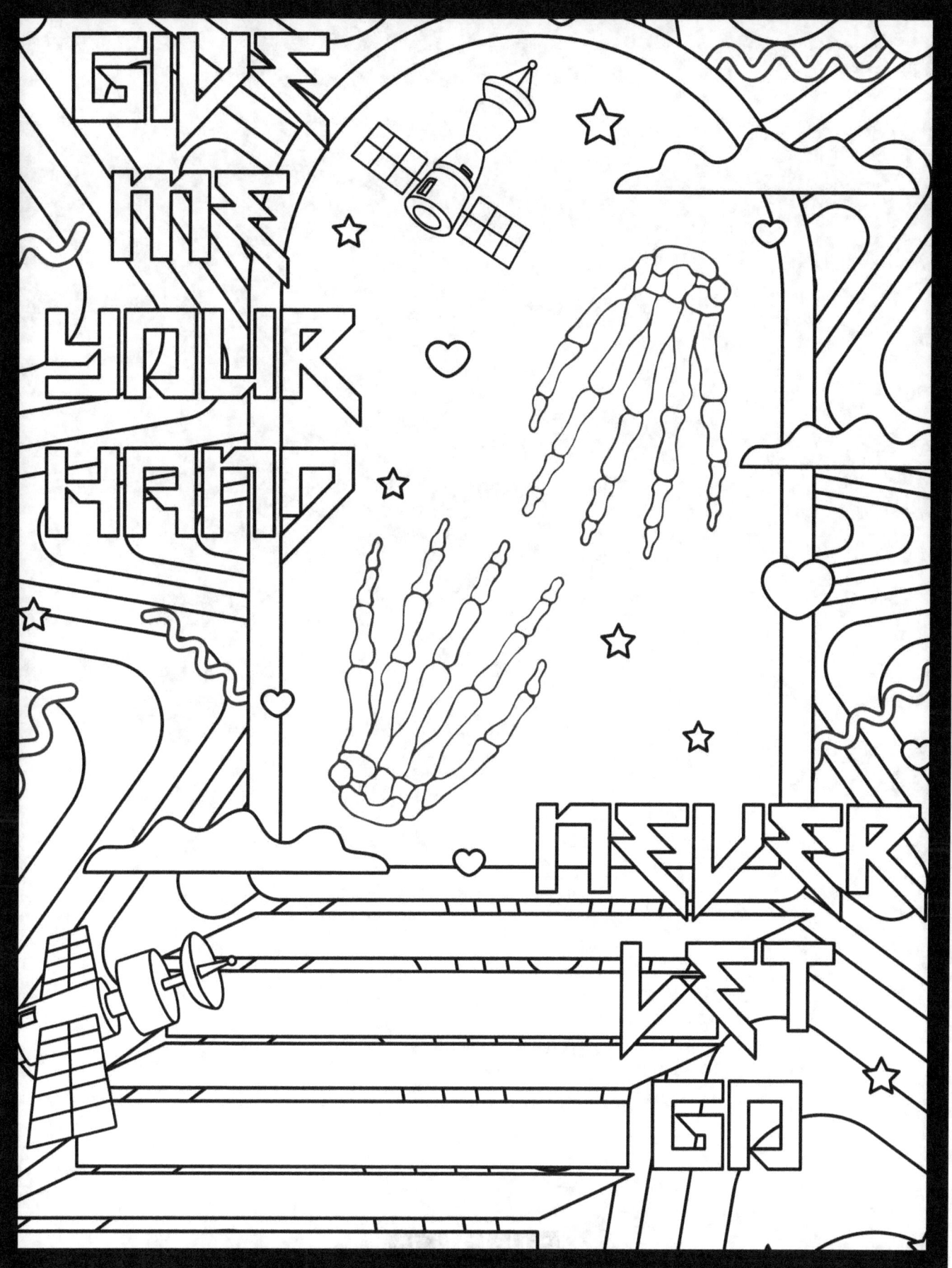

FOREVER

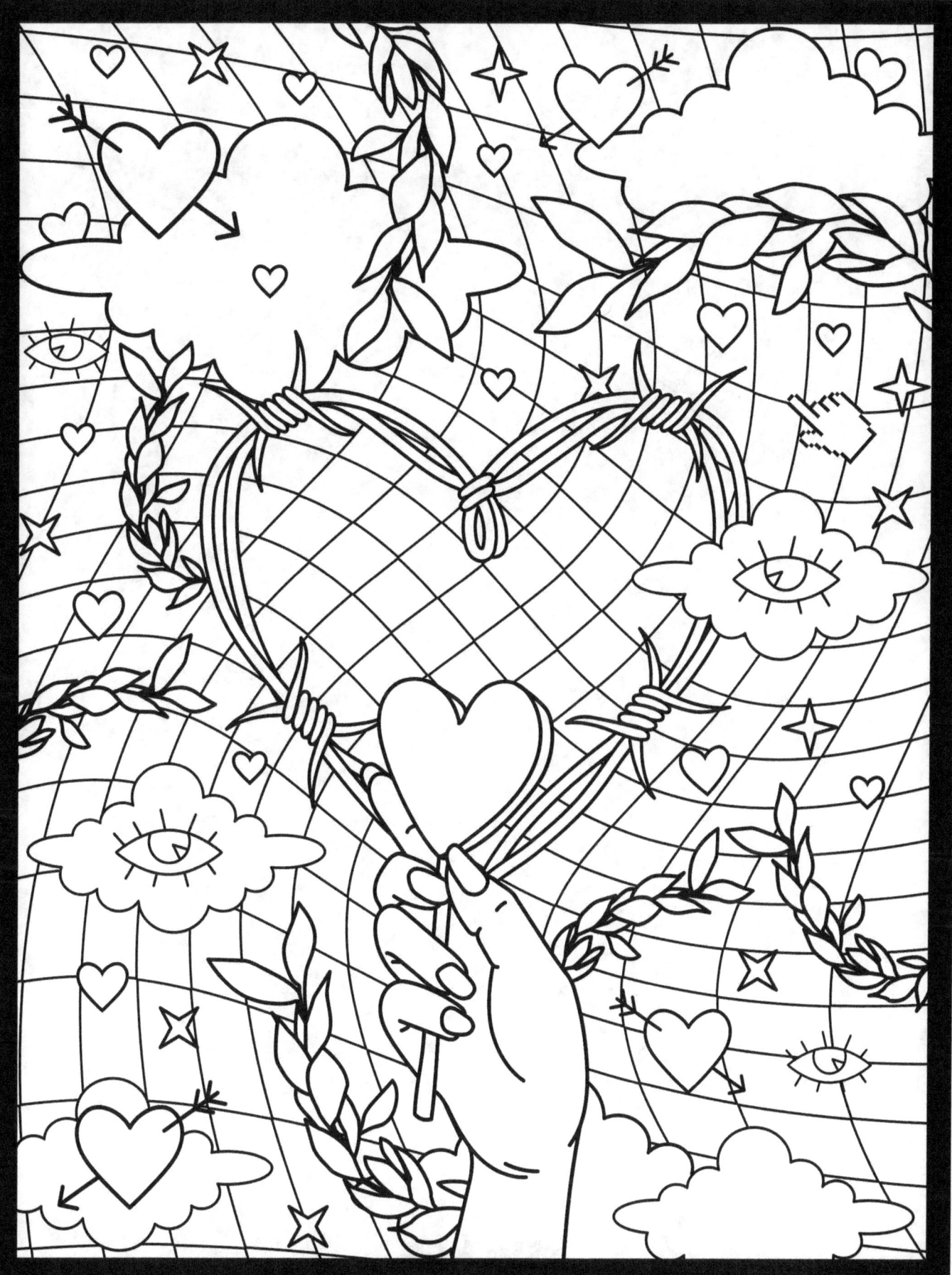

SUCKER

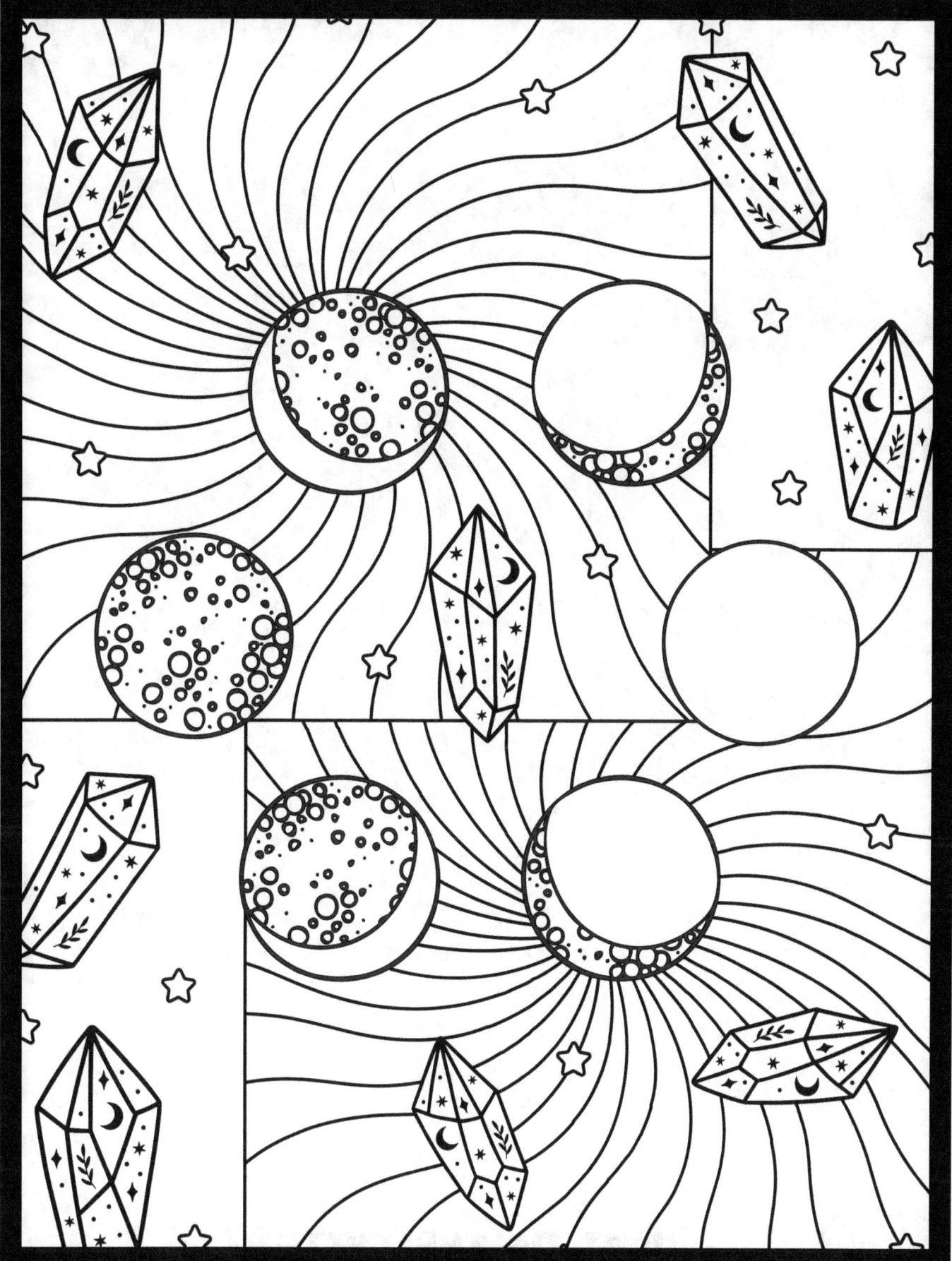

PART OF THE CYCLE

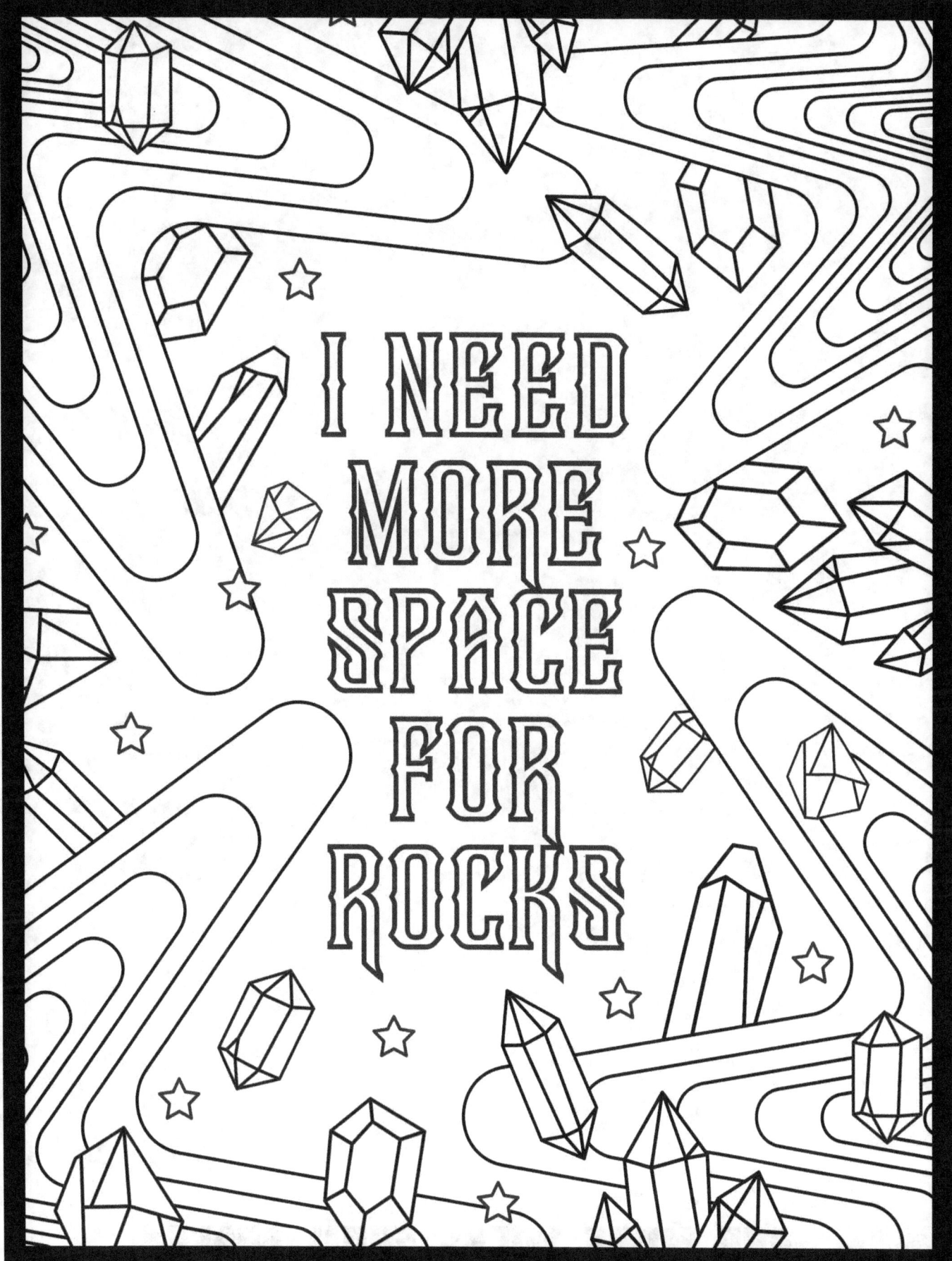

AND MORE ROCKS FROM SPACE

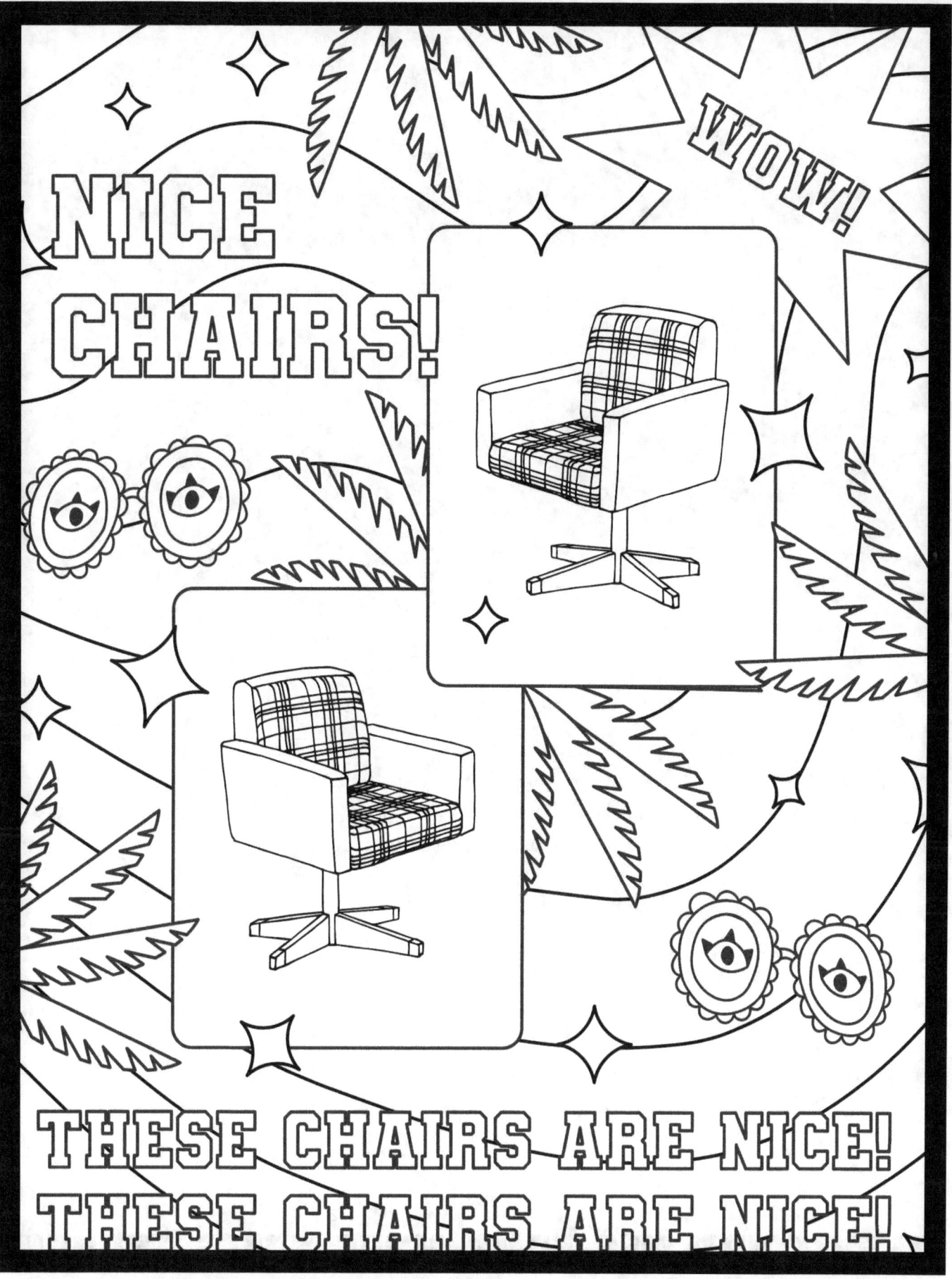

THEY COULD USE SOME MORE SPACE THOUGH

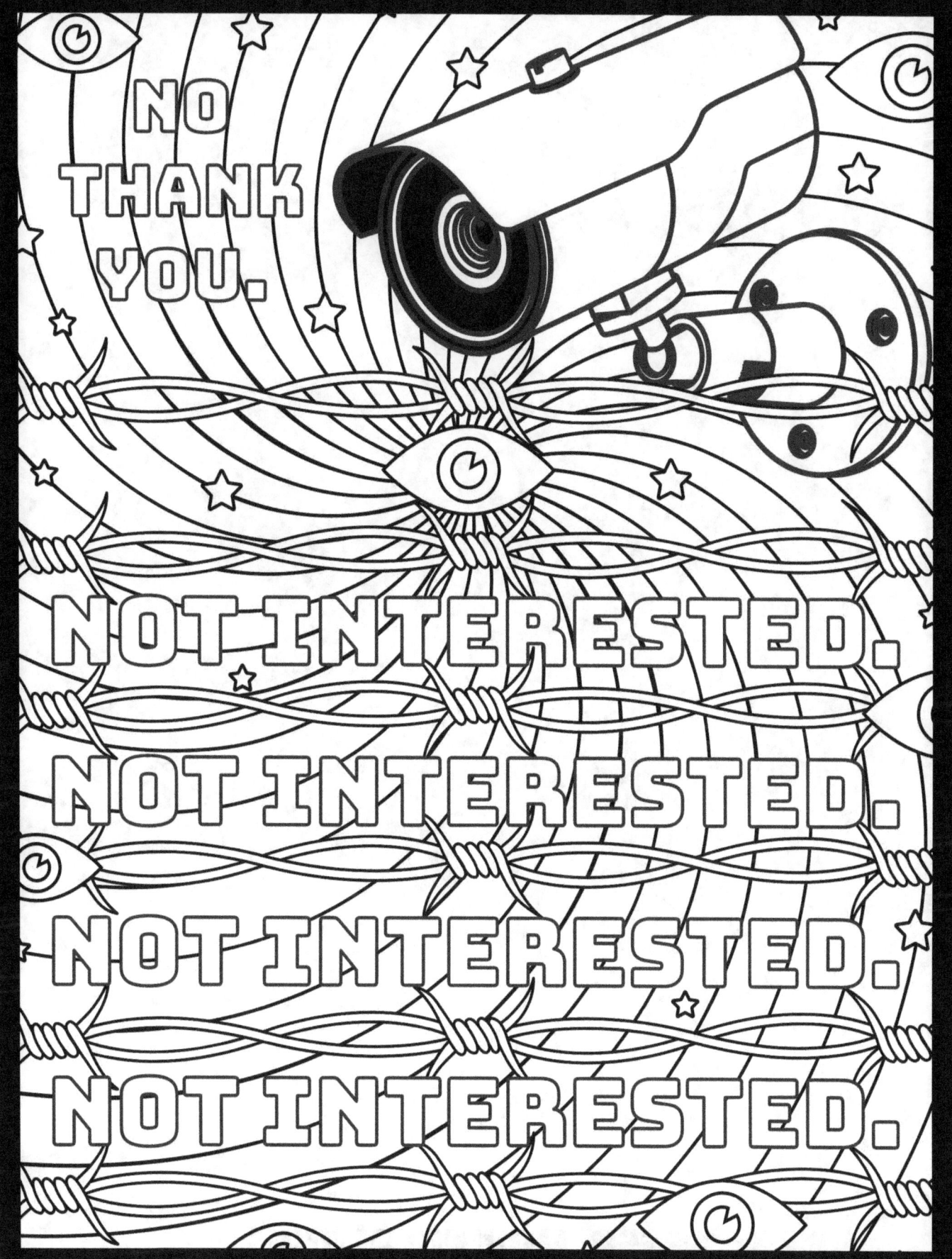

KEEP MOVING ALONG

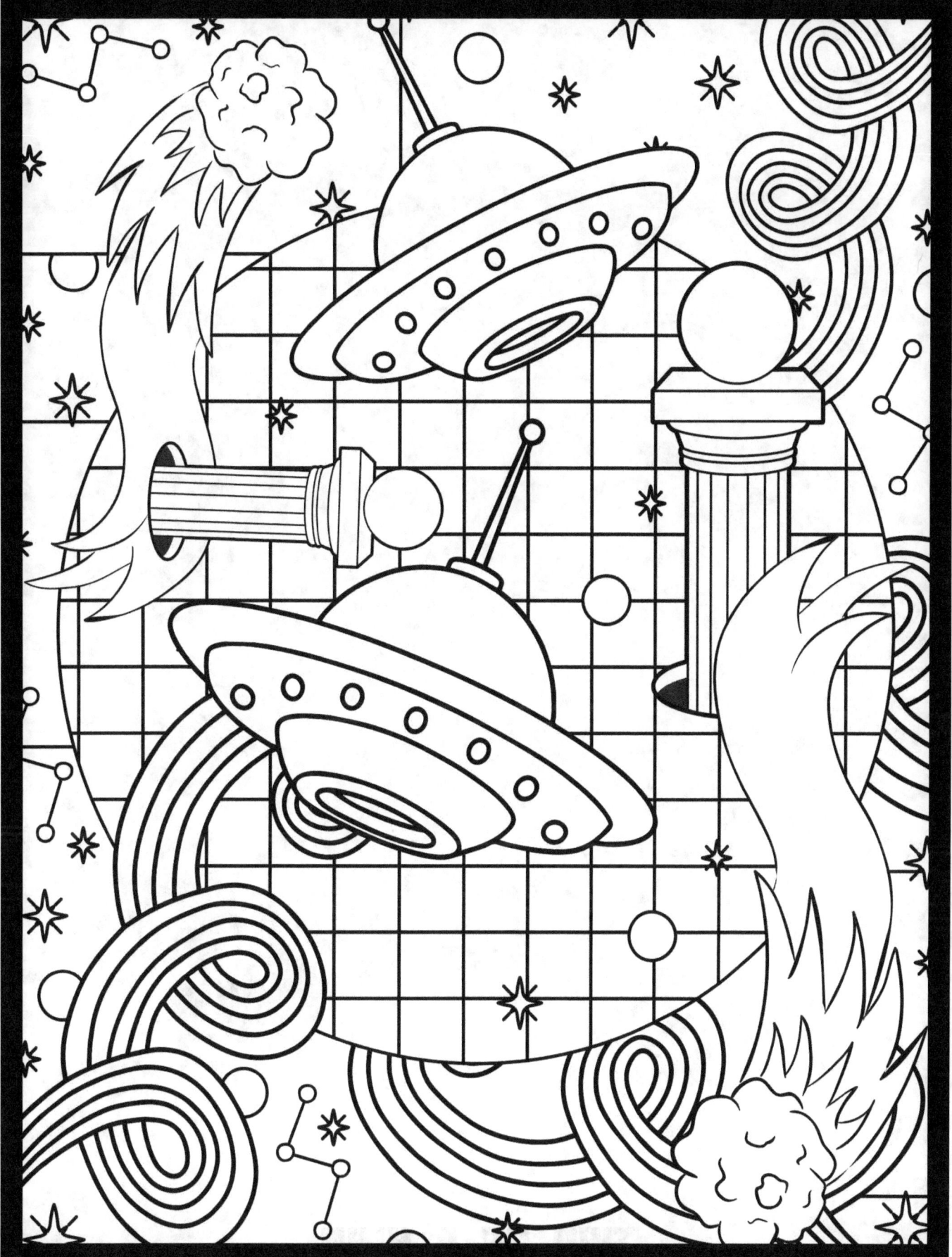

TWO OF A KIND

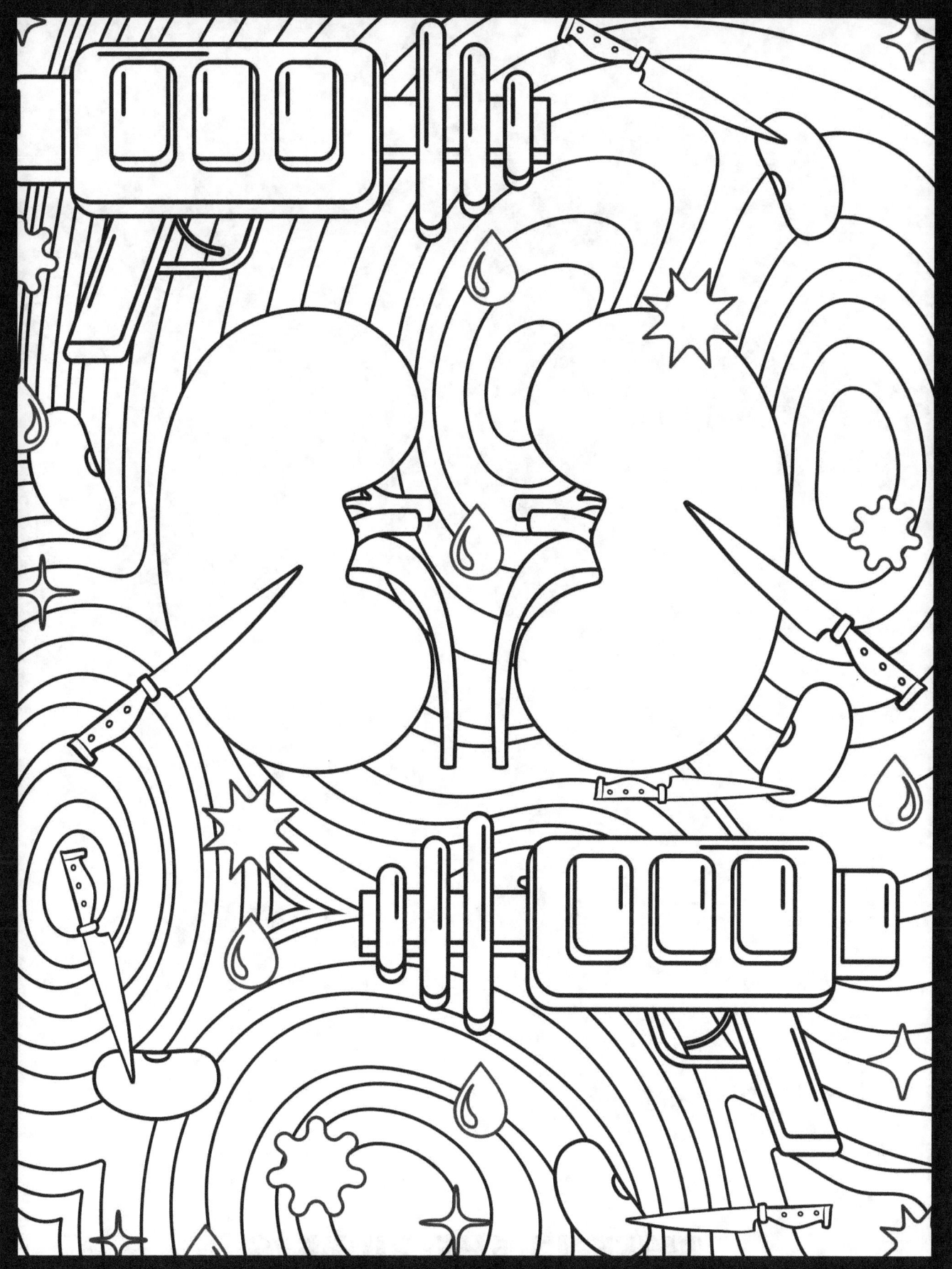

KNIFE IN THE KIDNEYS

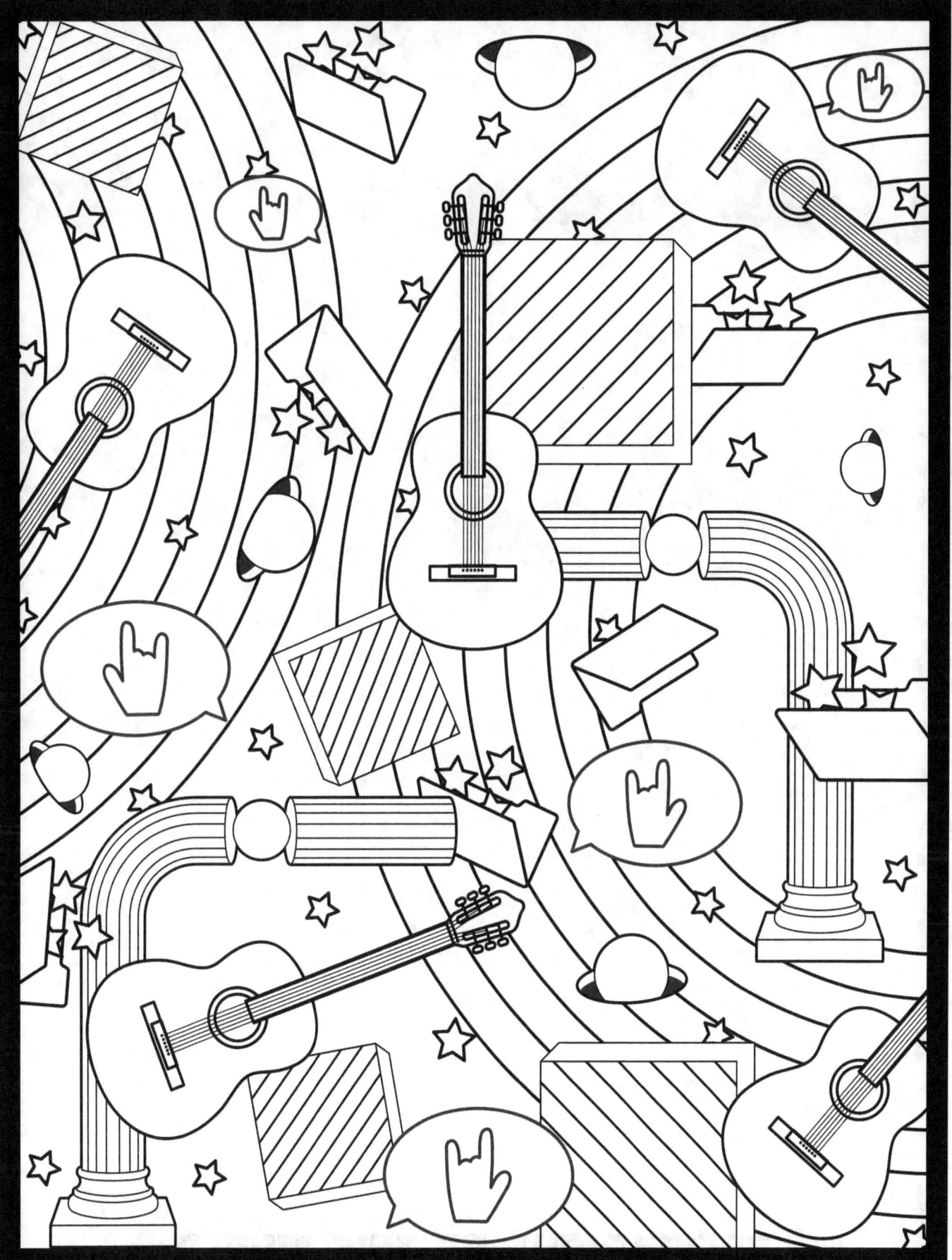

ROCKING OUT OF THIS WORLD

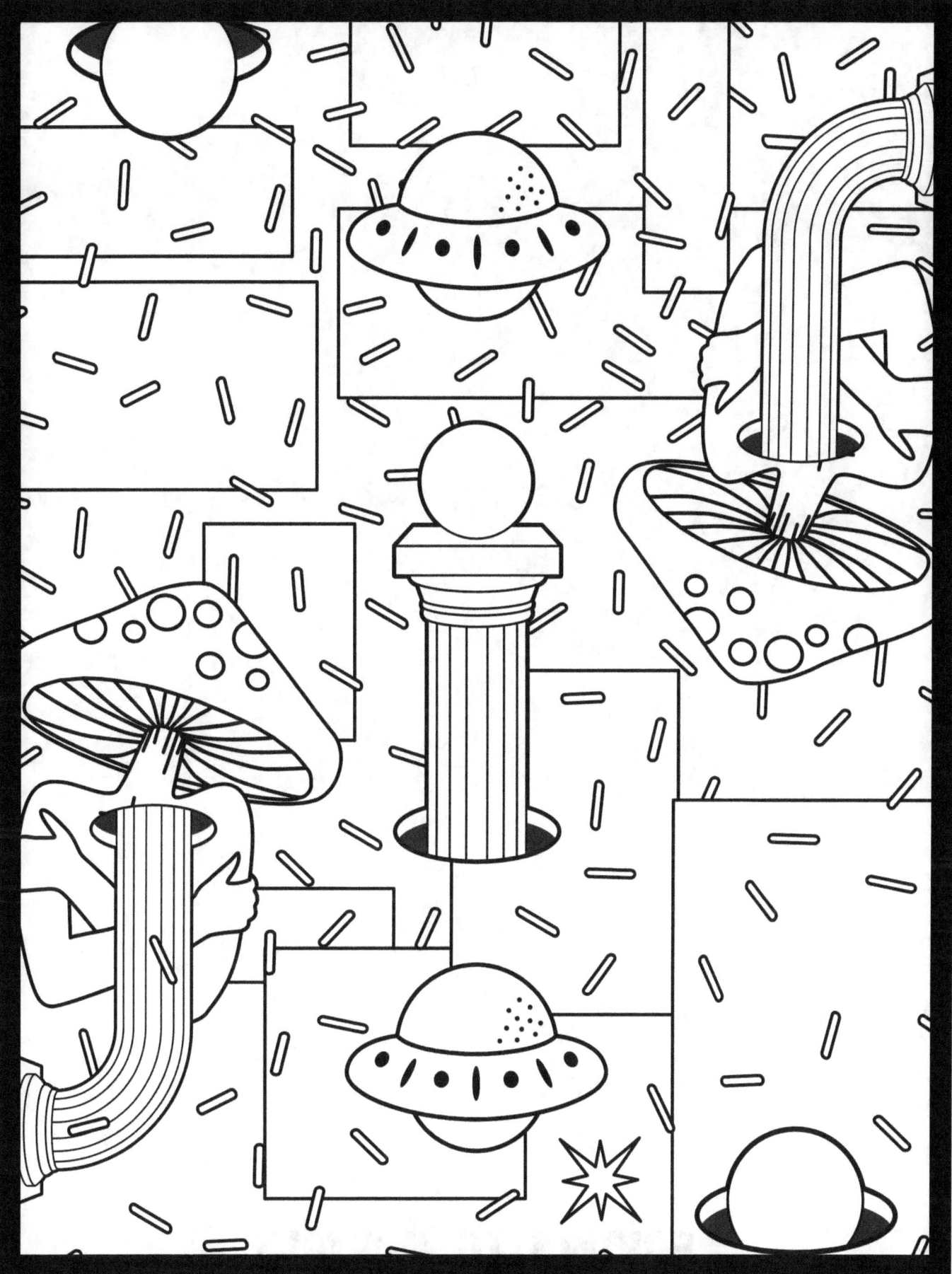

PORTALS TO MORTALS

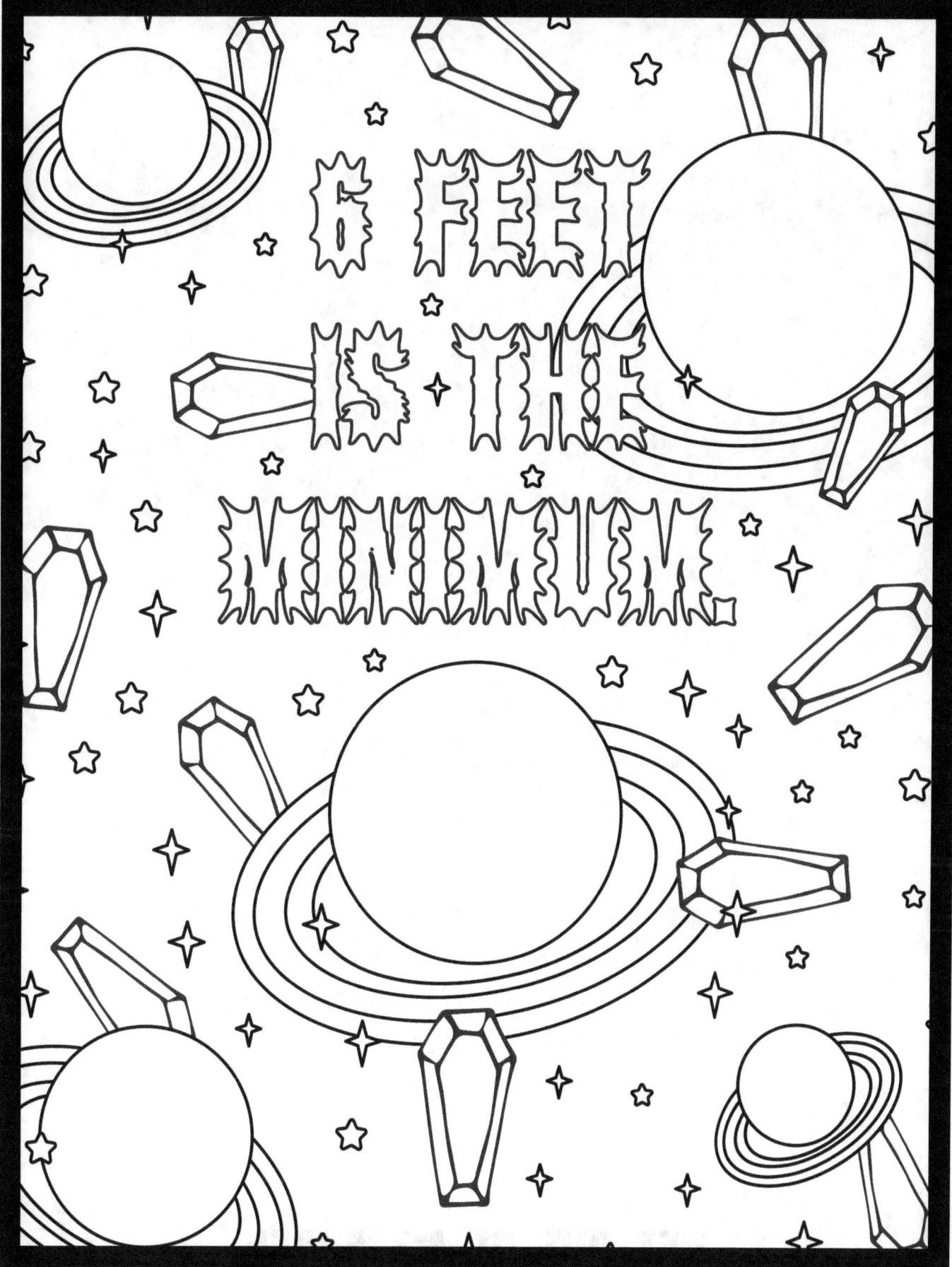

GET OUT OF MY SPACE

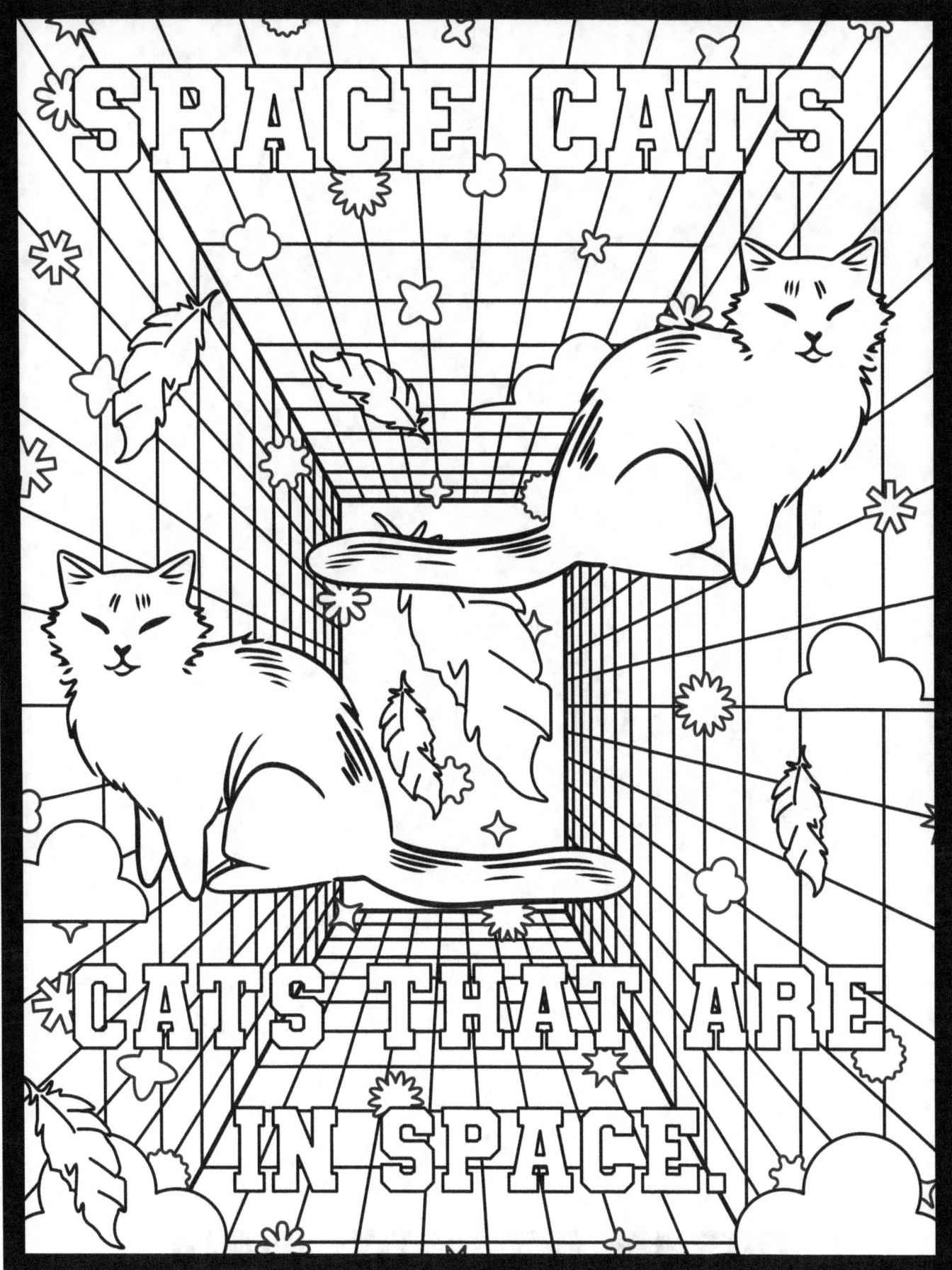

CATS ARE OUT OF THIS WORLD

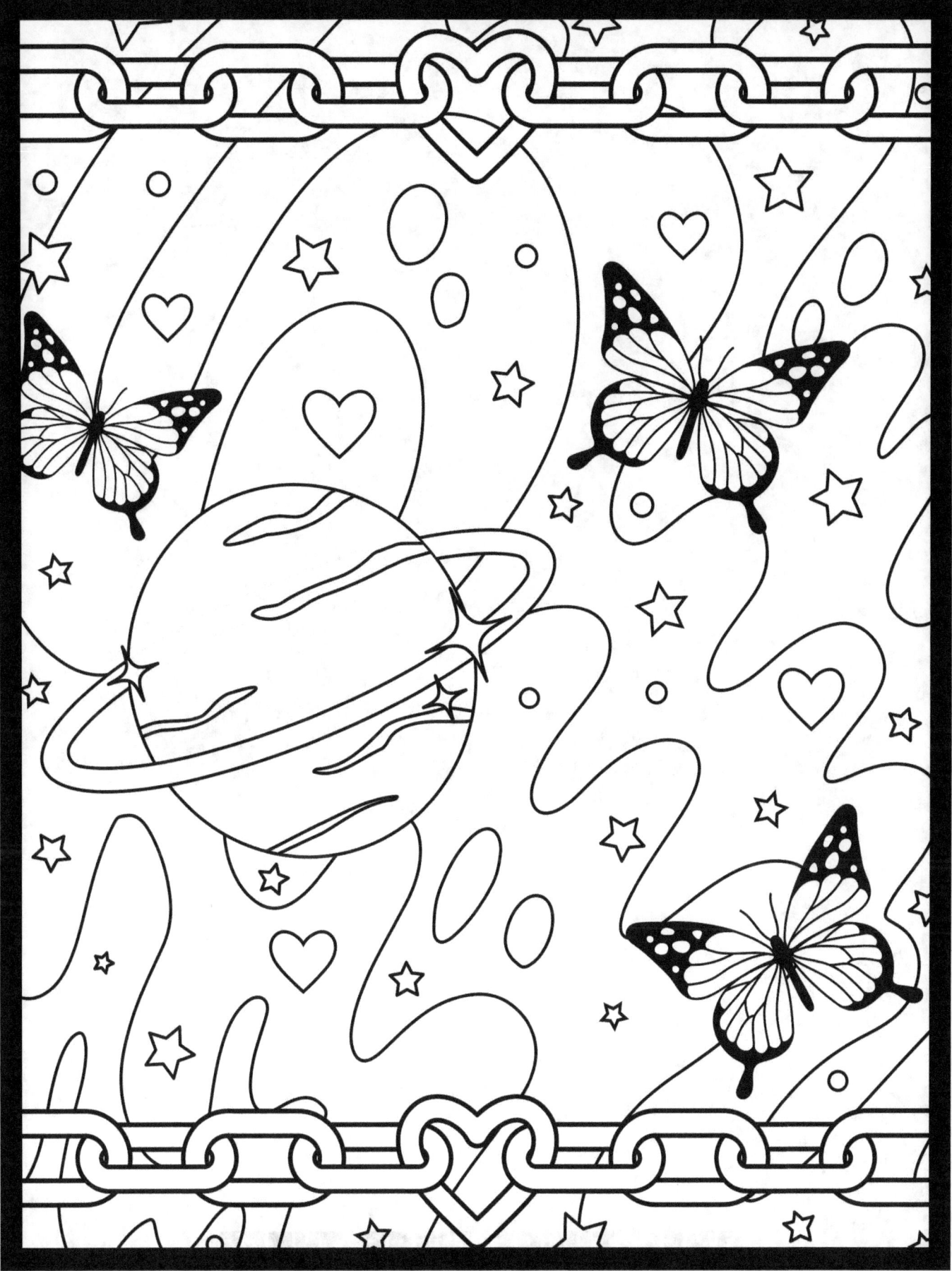

THEN THERE WERE THREE

GROWING GARDENS

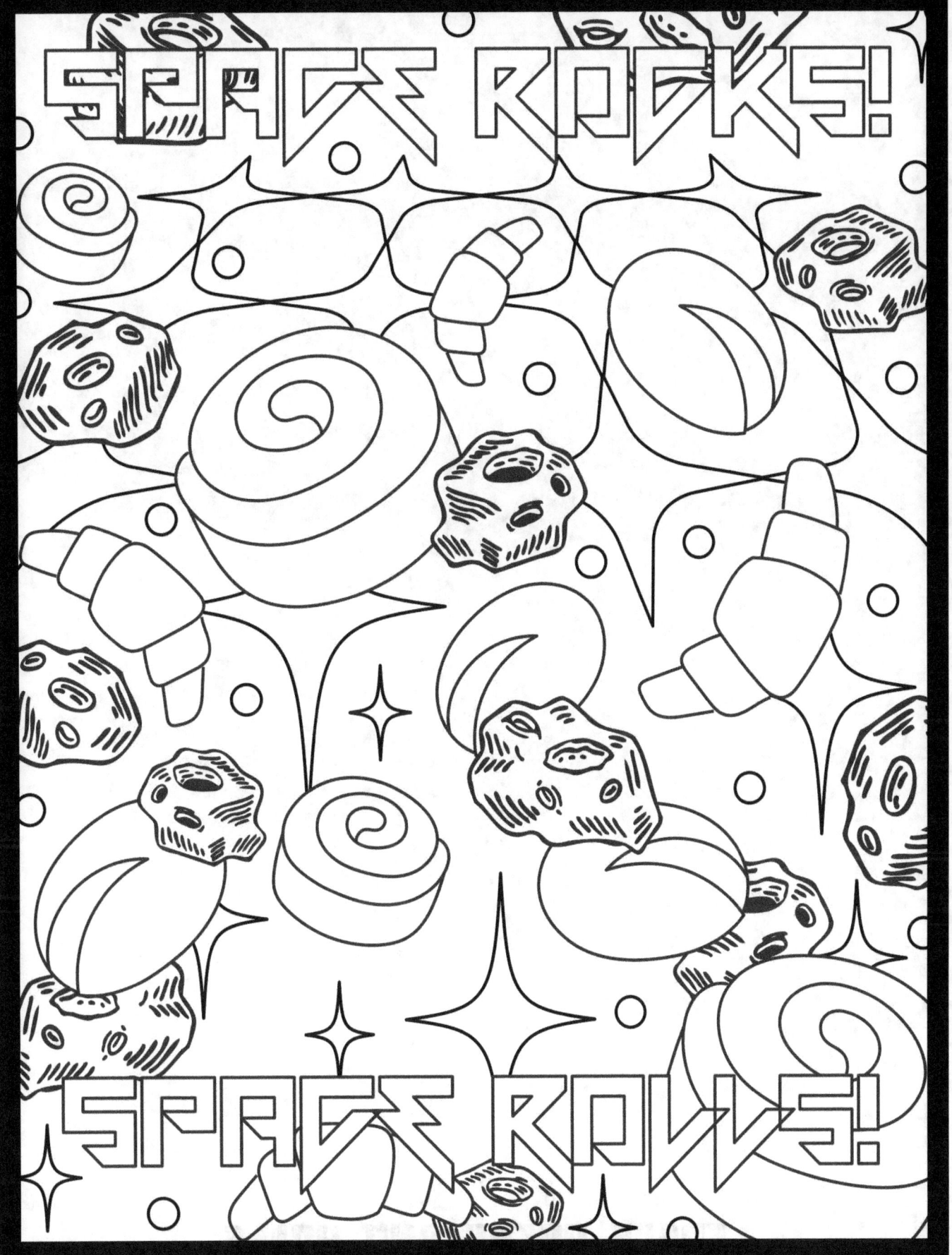

SPACE ROCKS AND ROLLS

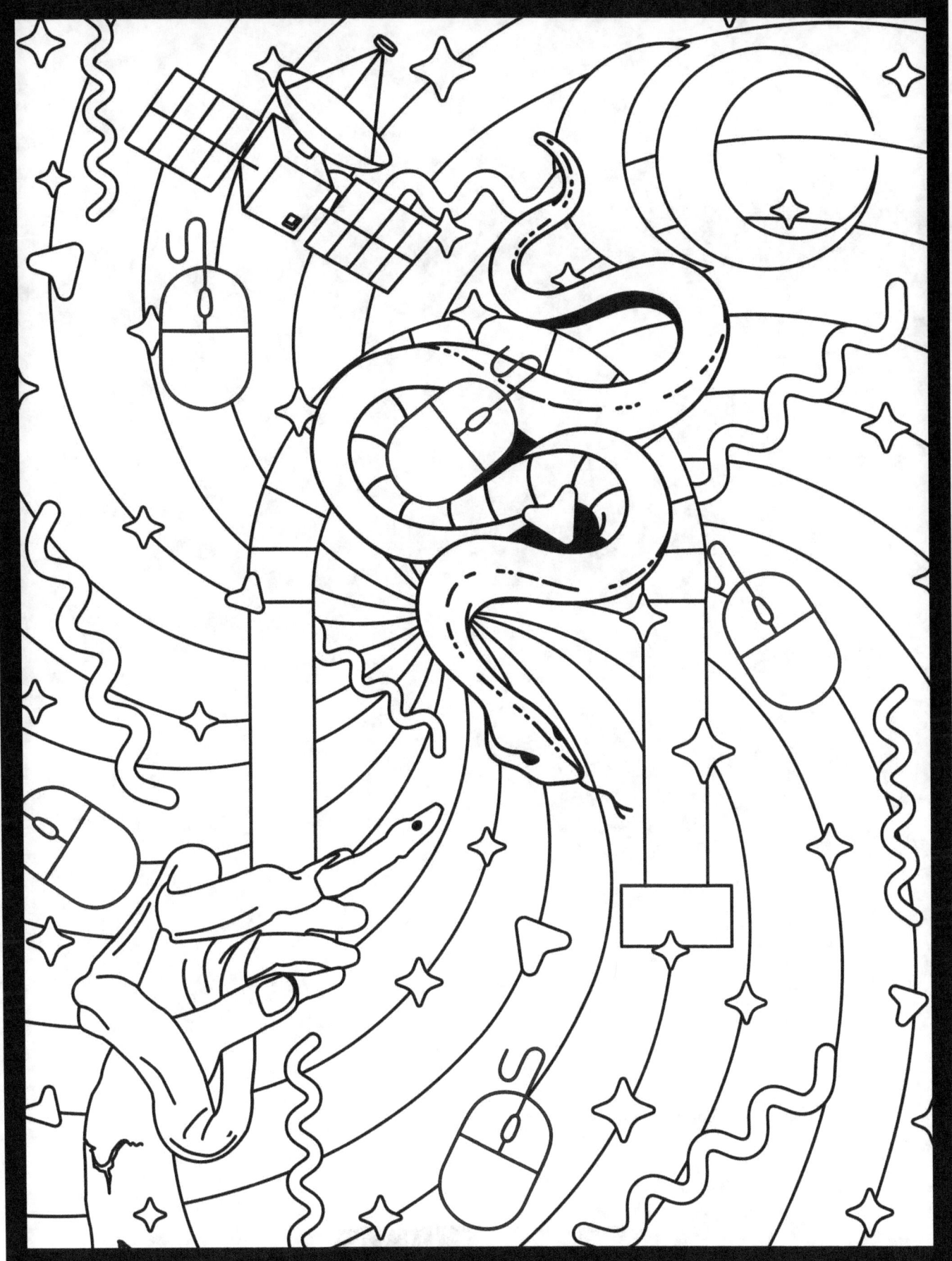

SPACE SNAKES

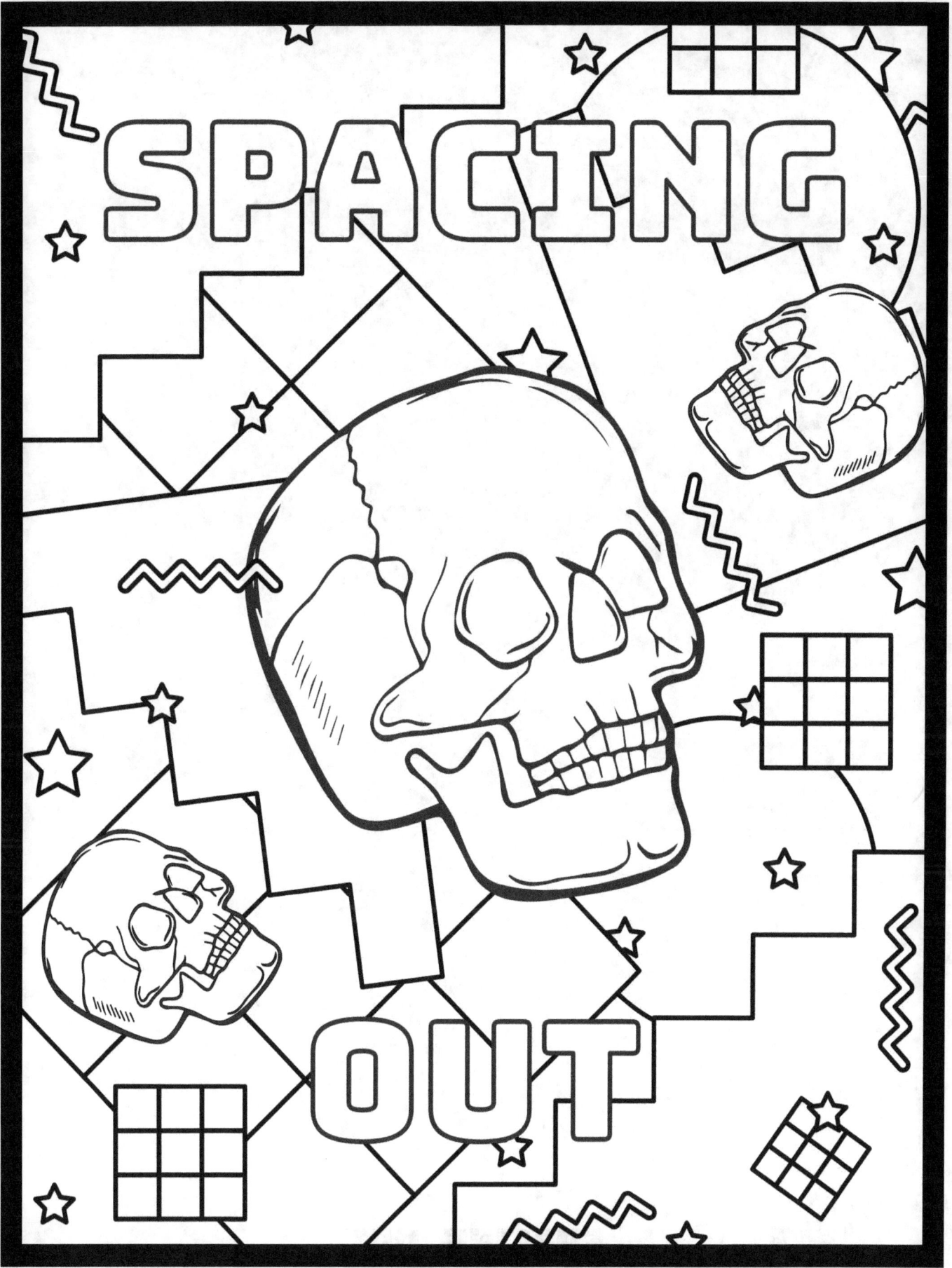

SPACING OUT

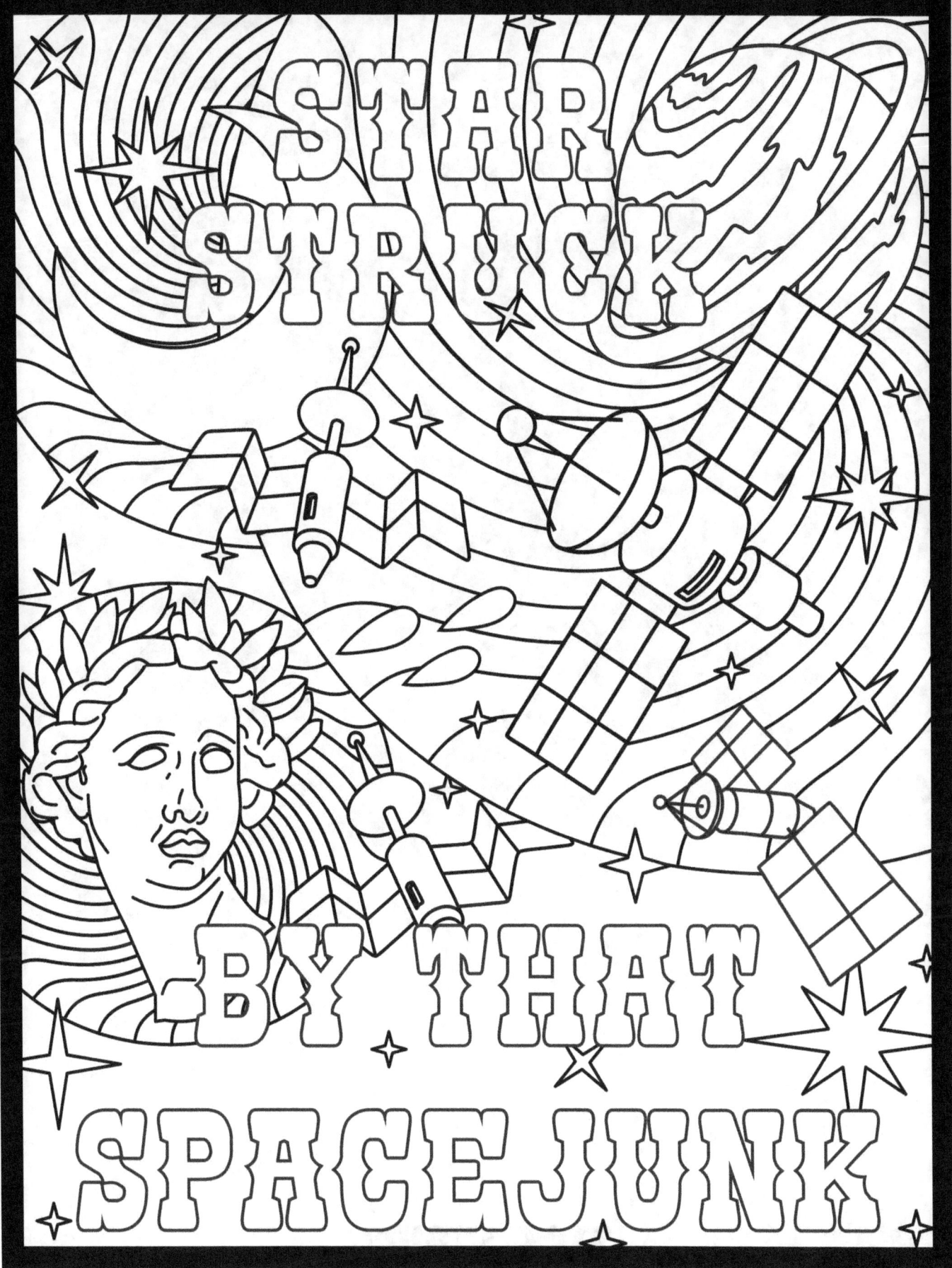

STAR STRUCK

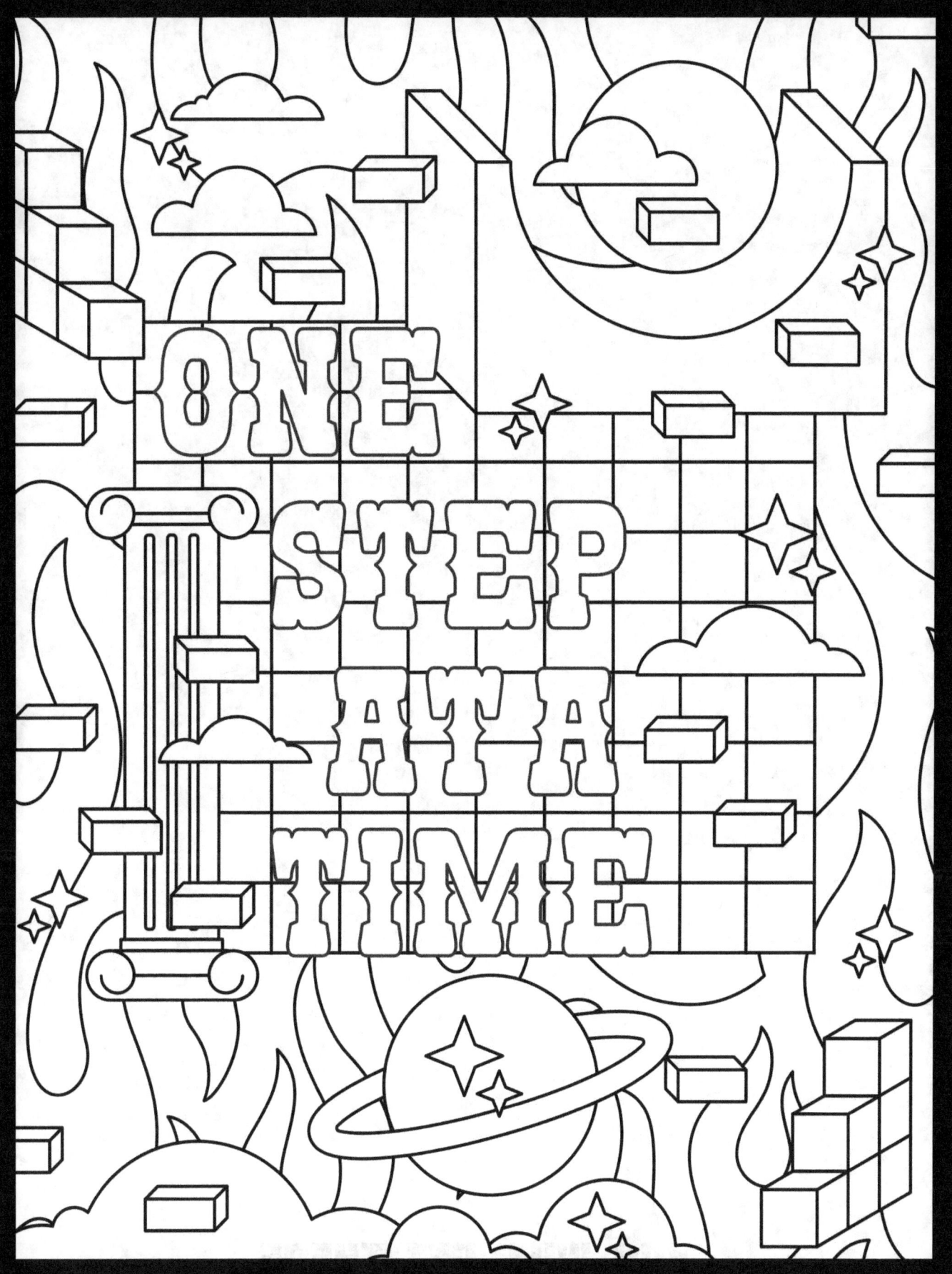

YOU WILL GET THERE

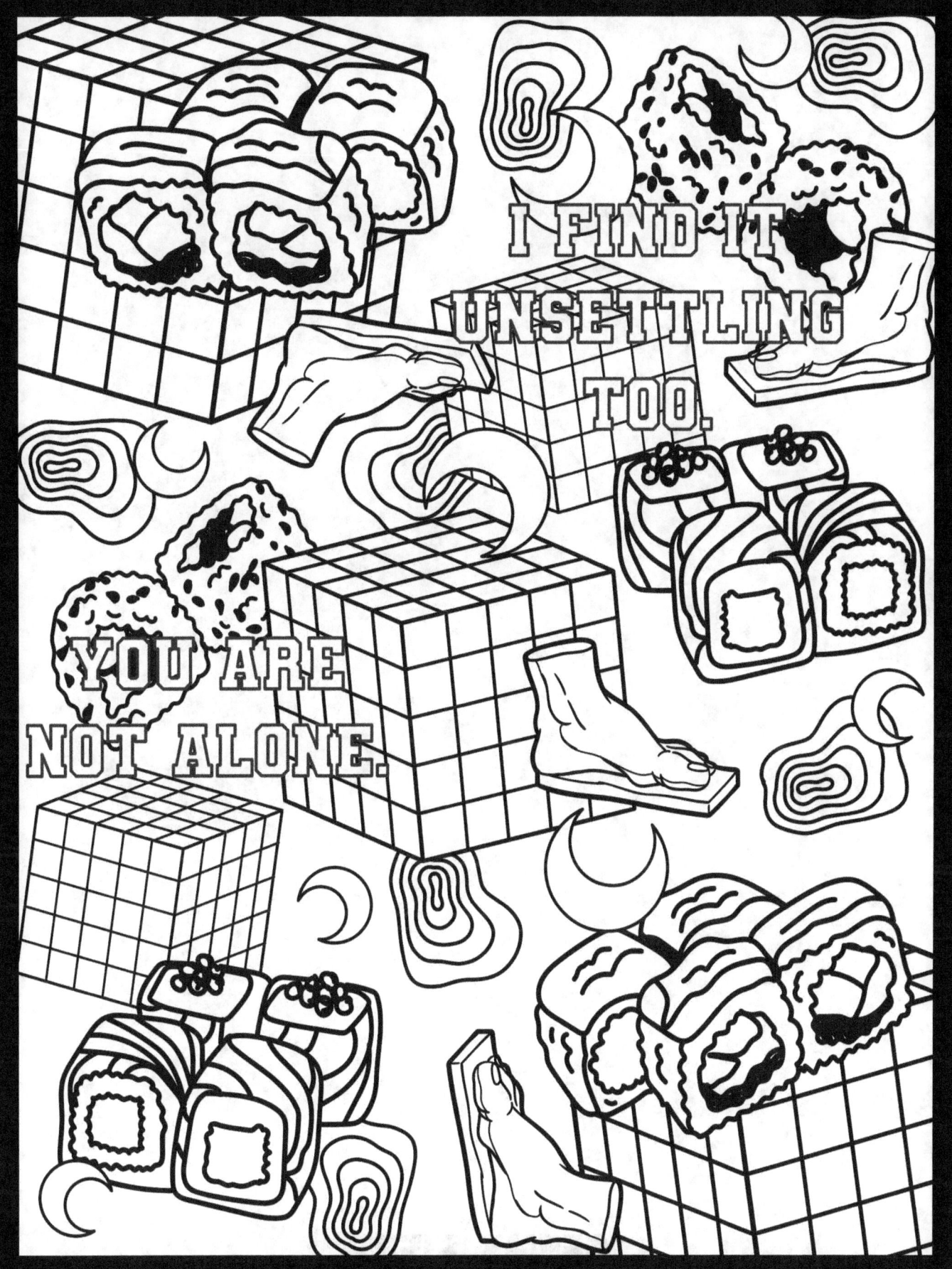

SEEMS FISHY

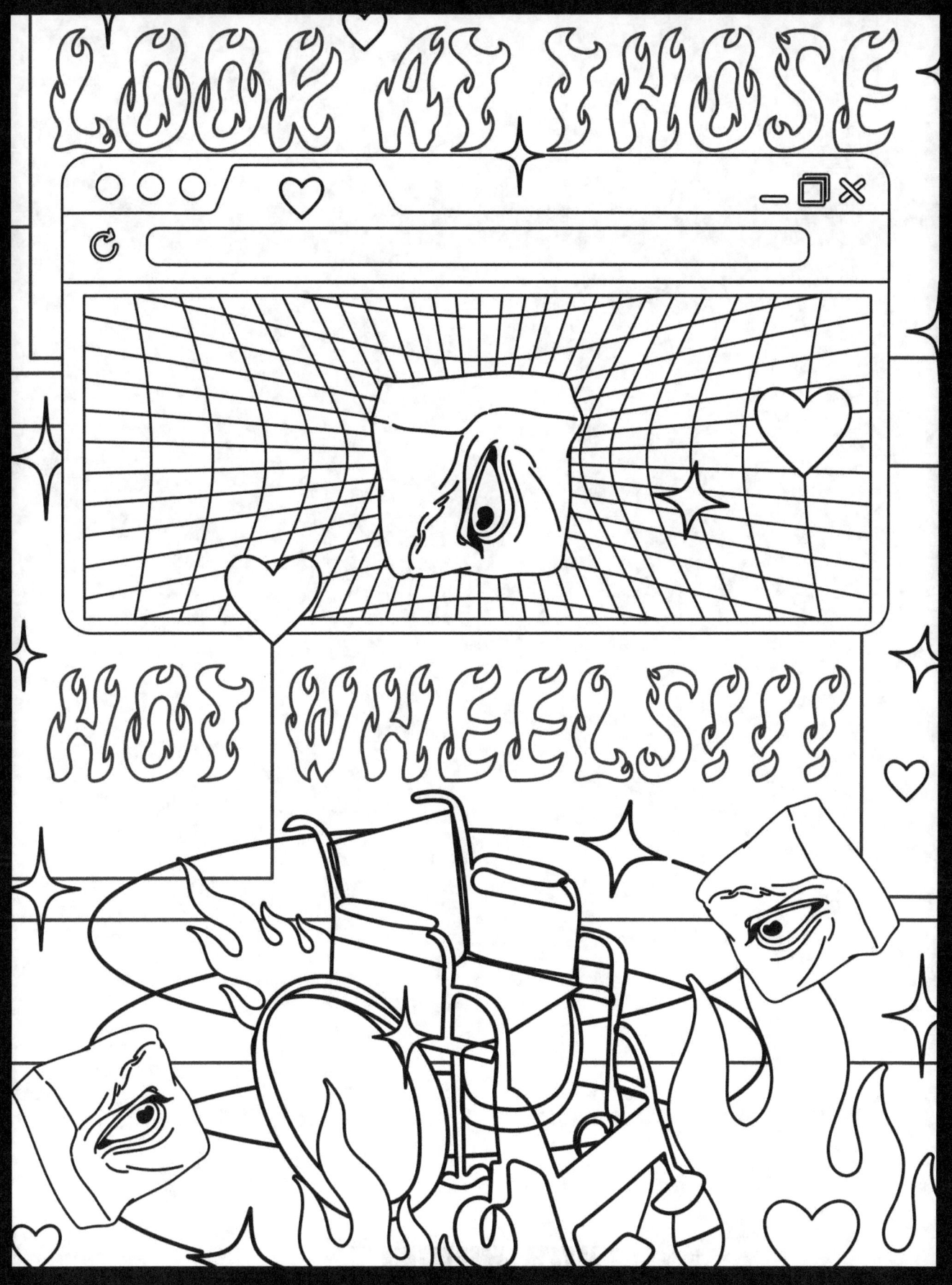

HOT WHEELS

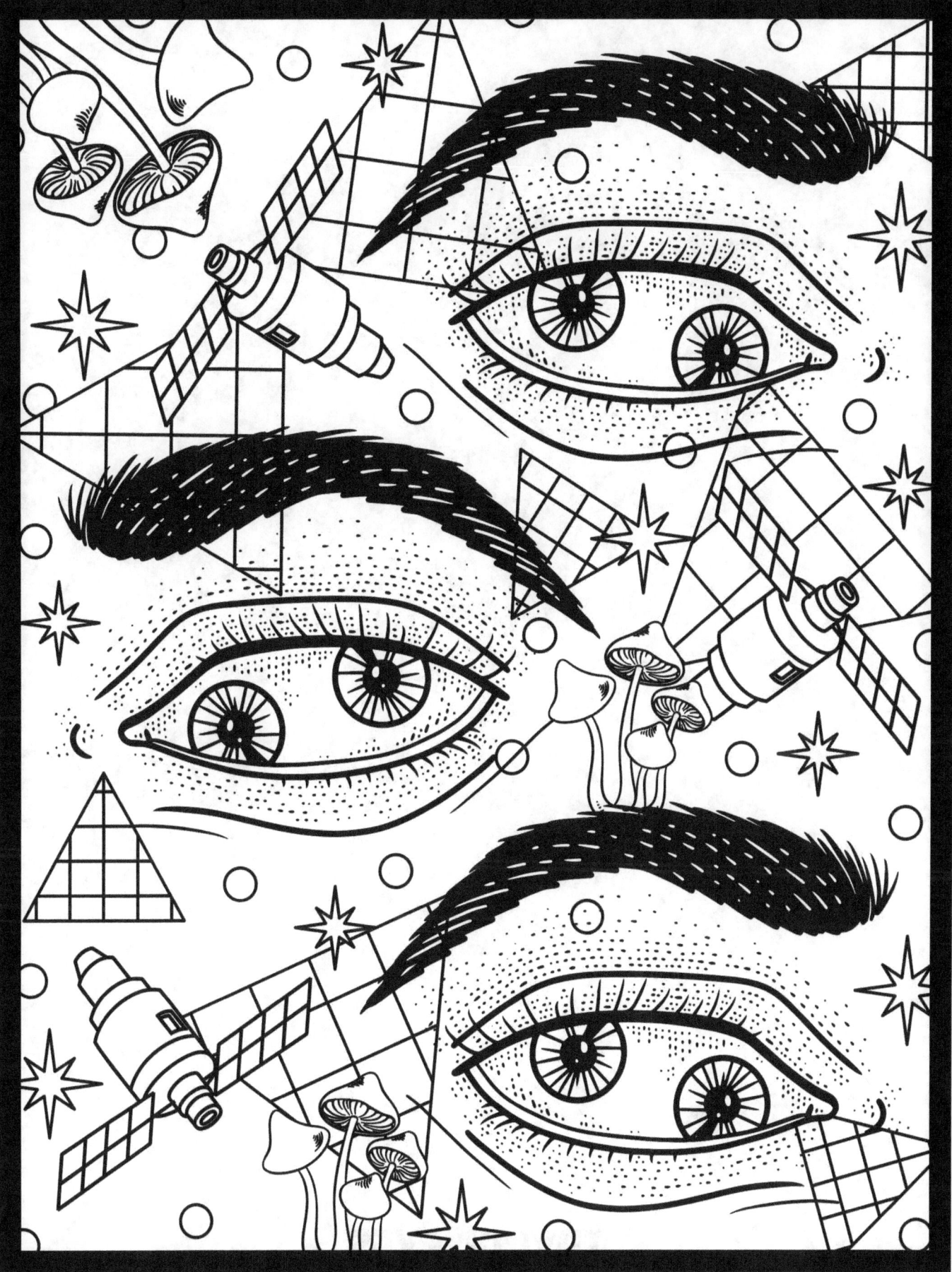

TRYING EYES

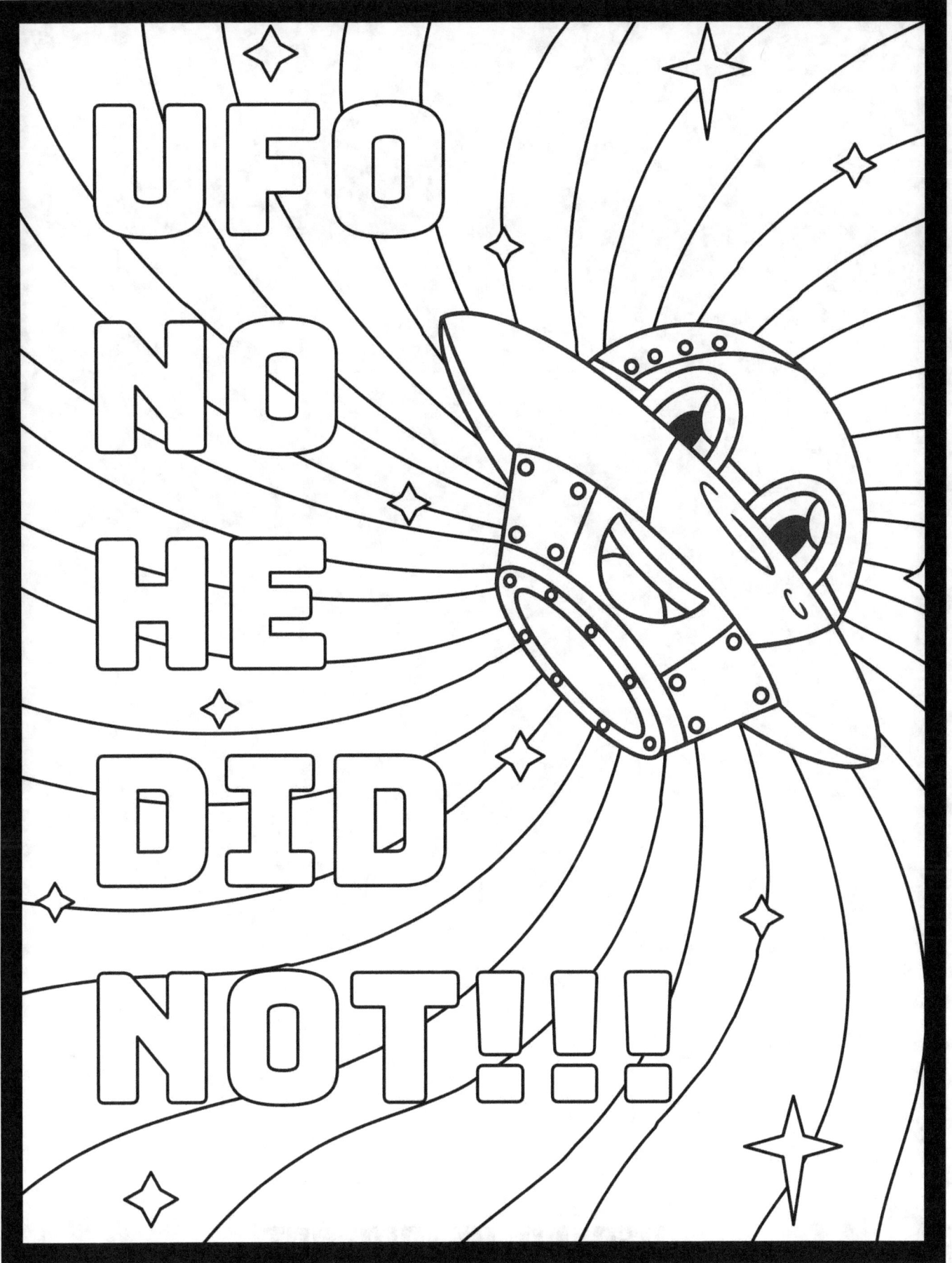

UFO NO HE DID NOT

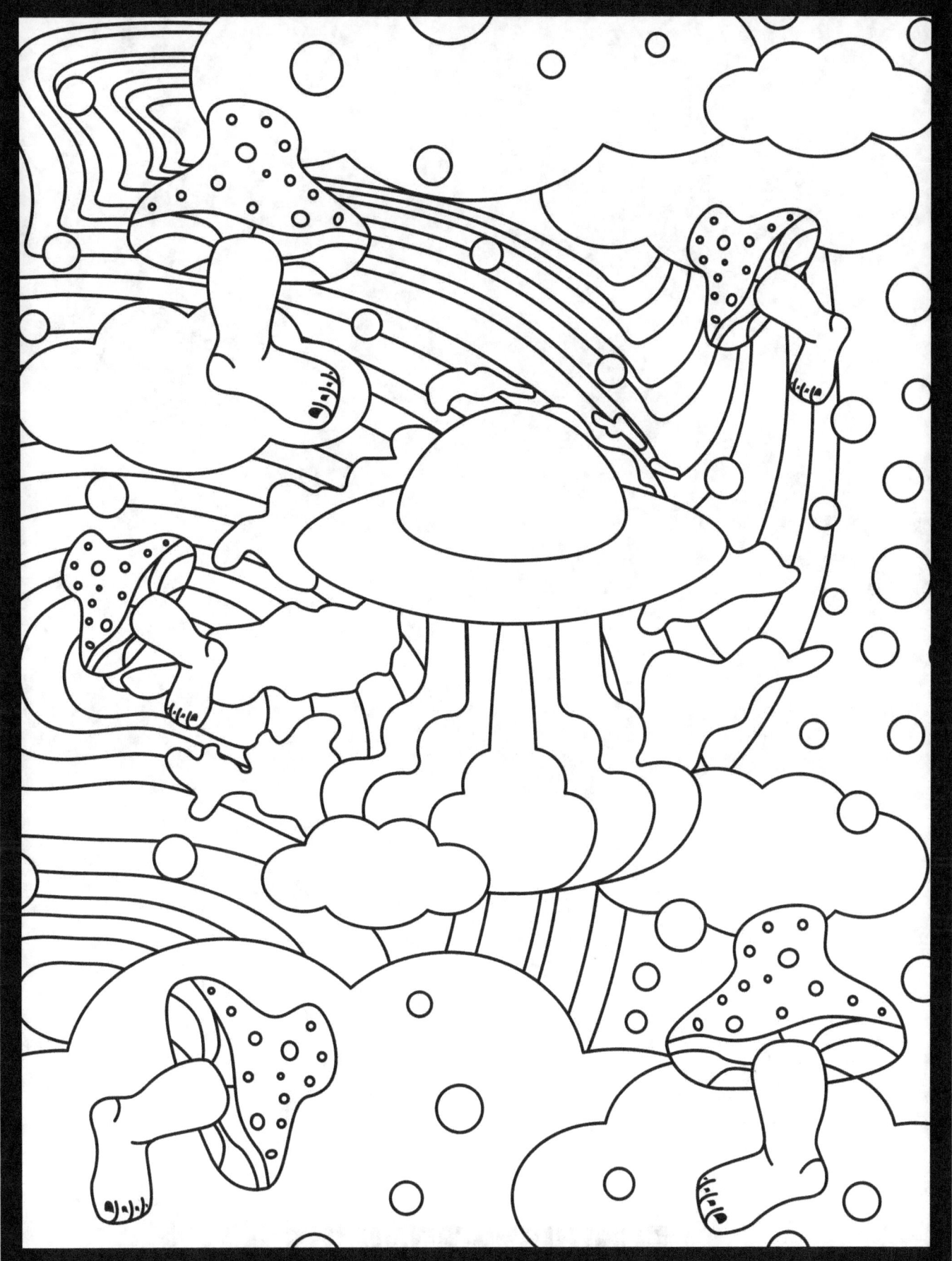

FUNGUS AMONG US

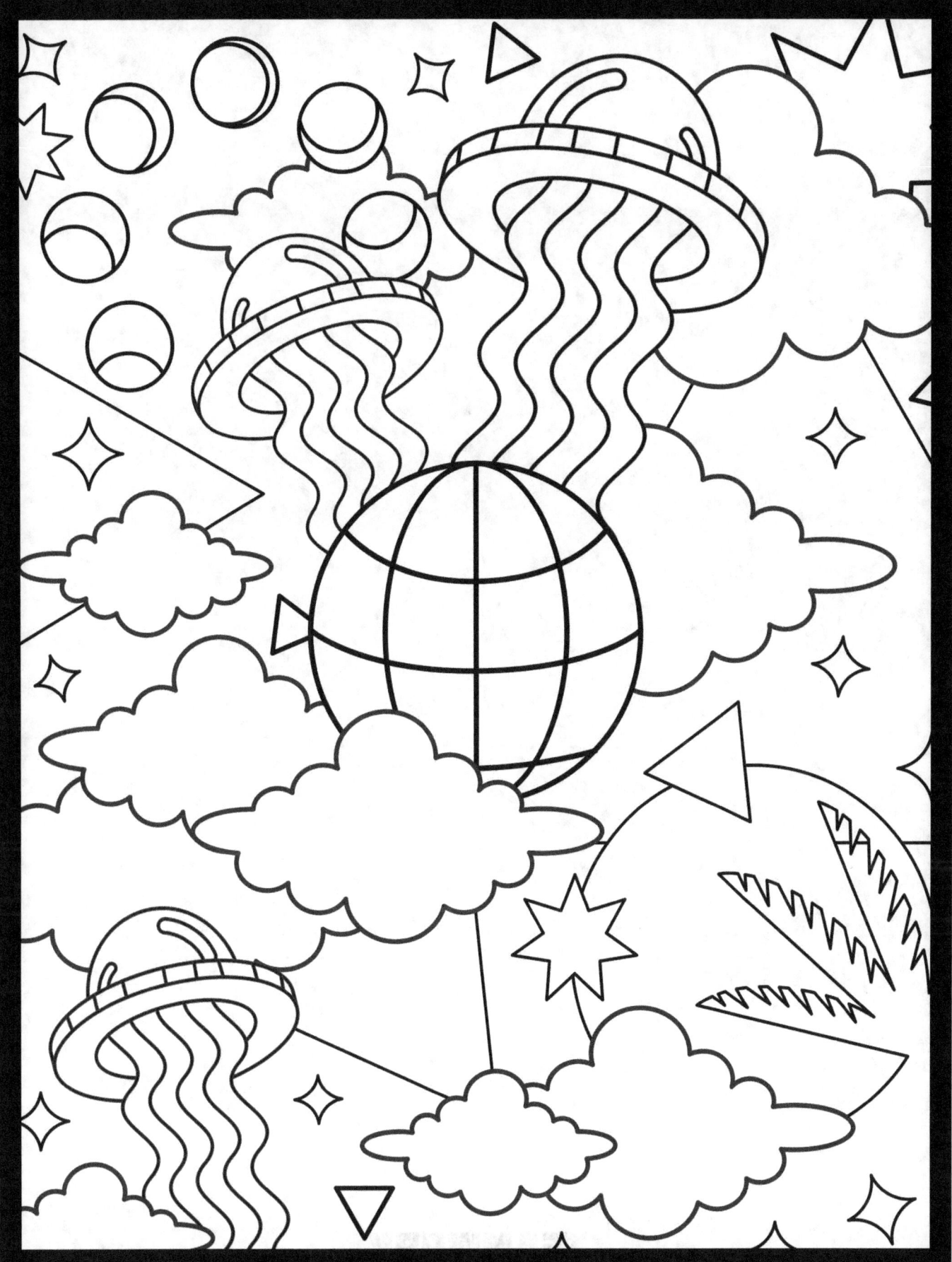

TEAMWORK

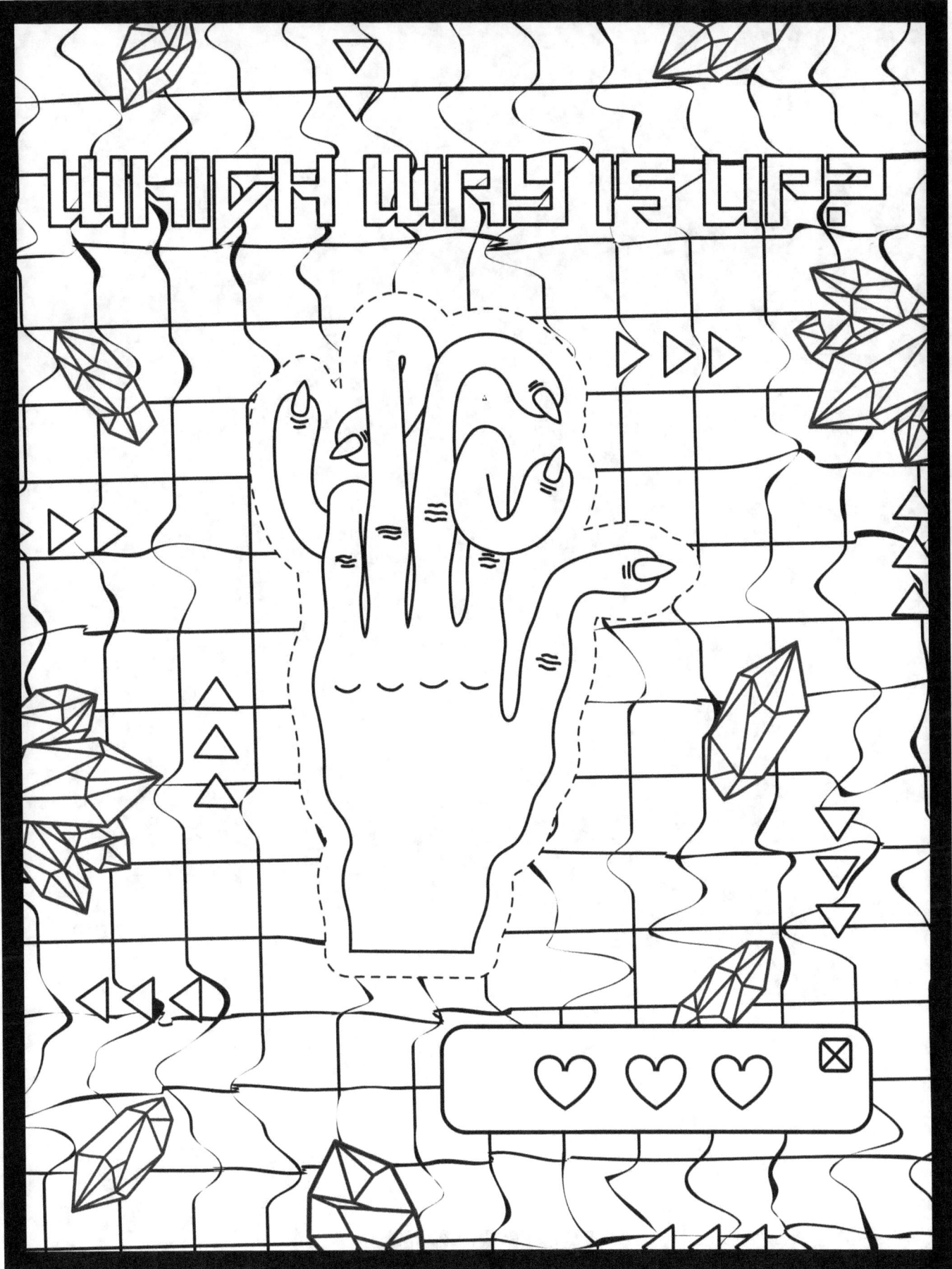

WHICH WAY

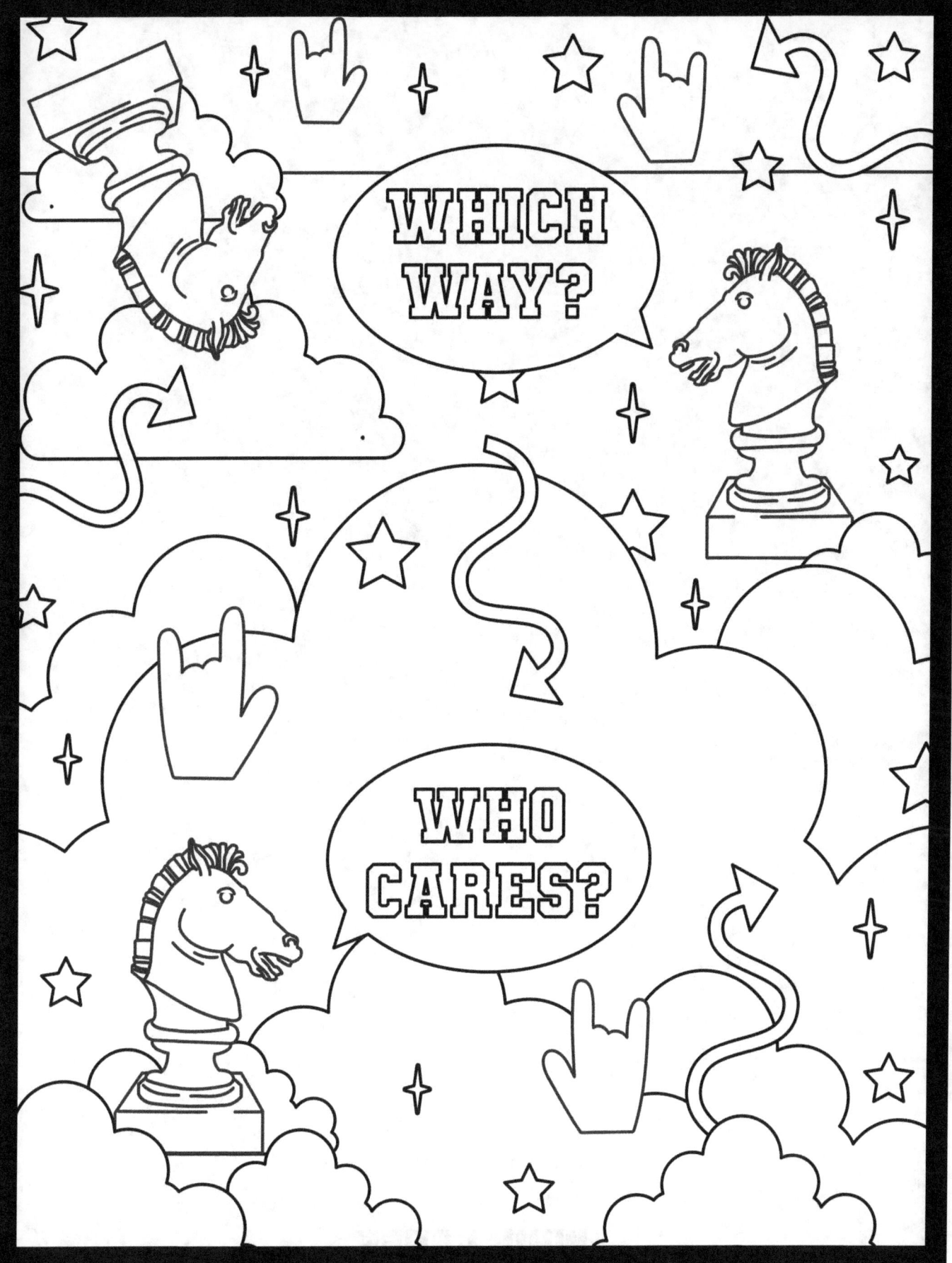

WHO CARES

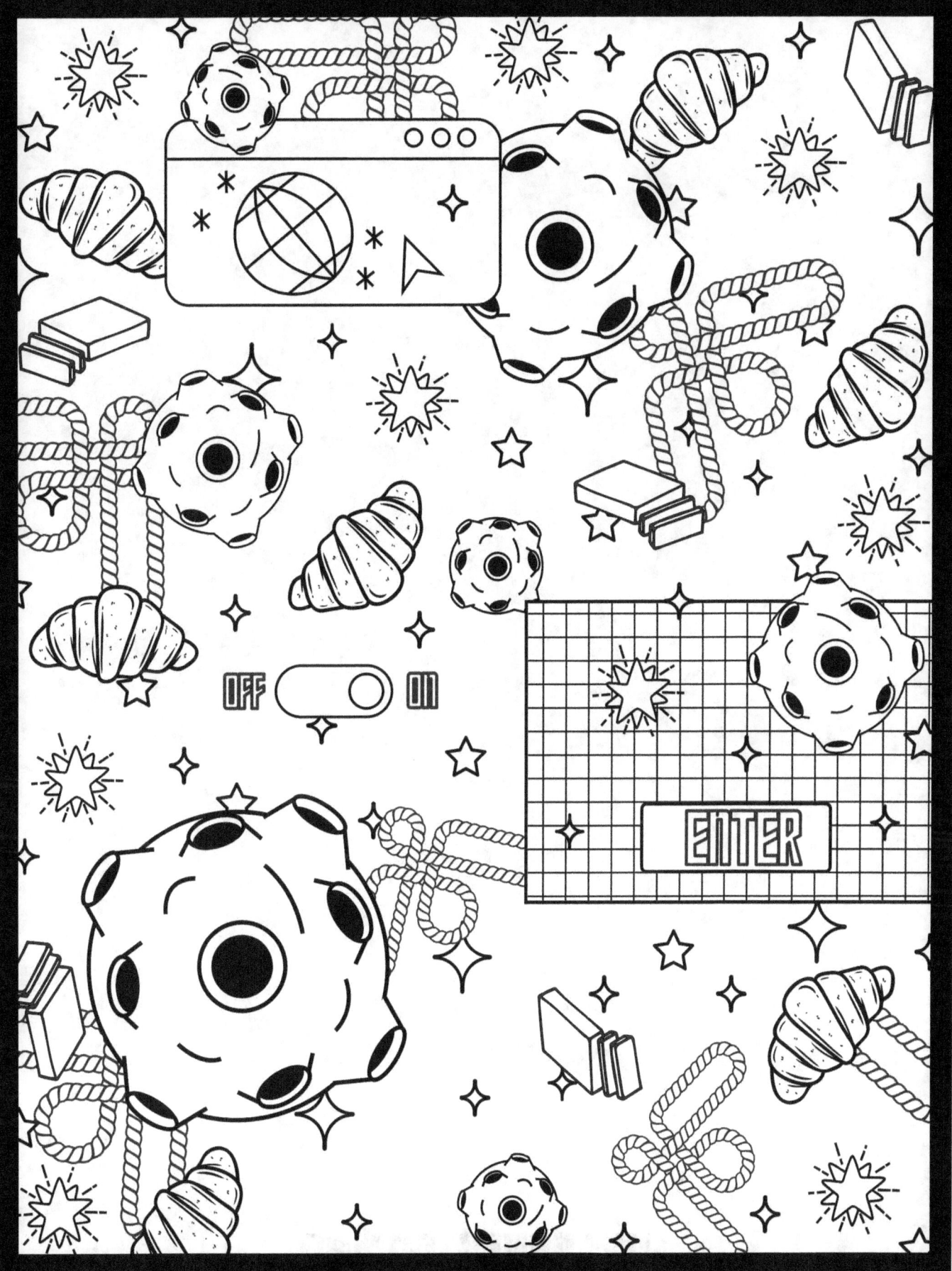

HEAVENLY COMBO

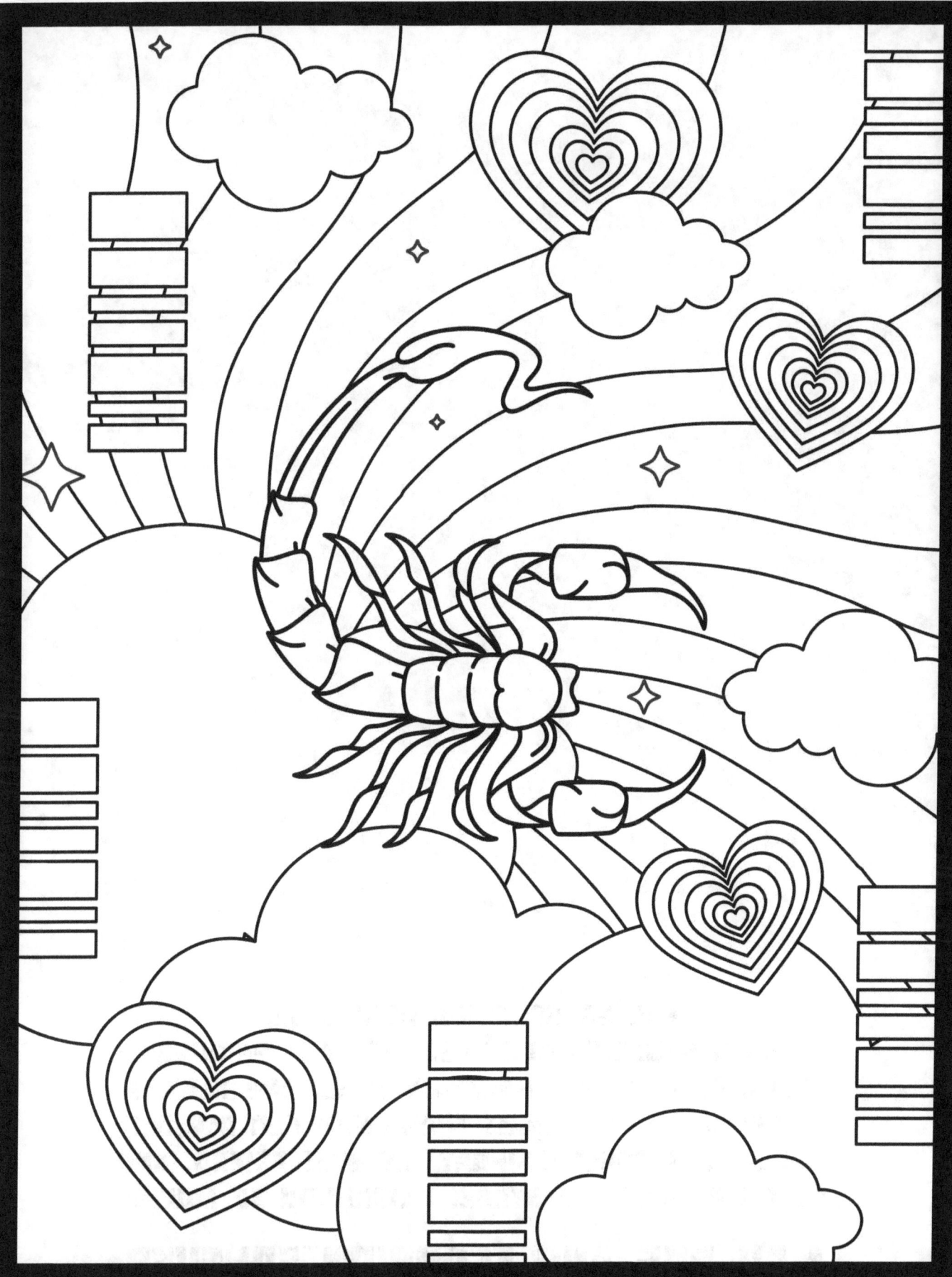

FOR MY SCORPION WITH LOVE.
FROM BRUSHING OUR TEETH IN NASA PARKING LOTS, CAMPING AT ABDUCTION SITES, AND ALWAYS LOOKING TO THE STARS! THANK YOU FOR ALWAYS BEING MY BIGGEST SUPPORT, MY BEST FRIEND, AND MY GREATEST ADVENTURE! I LOVE YOU SO MUCH.

MAD DOG AND SCORPION FOREVER

LOVE

www.ingramcontent.com/pod-product-compliance
Lightning Source LLC
Chambersburg PA
CBHW080504220526
45465CB00006B/2376